"As we remember these powerful stories of transformation, we celebrate that the breakdowns in our life are an opportunity for a break-through to more. Each one of us is called on our journey together to live what these stories call us to believe: that our lives are not for our own sake but for the sake of others."

— Fr. Christopher Keenan, OFM
Chaplain, Fire Department of New York

"On September 11 we saw the towers fall from my office window in Manhattan. We also were present as many people's lives and expectations were transformed by the experience of this huge communal tragedy. I served as Lutheran bishop in New York in the time of this wound to our city's soul. Wendy Healy served at my side as the communication's director for our Office of Bishop in the Metropolitan New York Synod of the Evangelical Lutheran Church in America. She captured the stories in the days following the attack. As she encountered many whose lives were altered forever, I observed that Wendy herself embodied a life and vocation in transition, seared by the pain of so many in this time of tragedy. Her own story, her own tranformation is embedded in the stories she tells, among them, the story of my own son Jeremy. It is now ten years later. I am grateful to Wendy Healy for documenting the grace of transformation that rises out of chaos and tragedy. Ten years later she is still telling the story of growth and transformation rising from Ground Zero."

— The Rev. Dr. Stephen Paul Bouman,
Former Bishop of the Metropolitan New York Synod
of the Evangelical Lutheran Church in America
Executive Director of Congregational and Synodical Mission, ELCA

*Peace*

*Willard W.C. Ashley Sr.*

# LIFE IS TOO SHORT

*Stories of Transformation
and Renewal after 9/11*

## WENDY STARK HEALY

iUniverse, Inc.
Bloomington

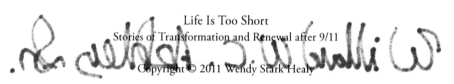

Life Is Too Short

Stories of Transformation and Renewal after 9/11

Copyright © 2011 Wendy Stark Healy

iUniverse books may be ordered through booksellers or by contacting:

iUniverse
1663 Liberty Drive
Bloomington, IN 47403
www.iuniverse.com
1-800-Authors (1-800-288-4677)

Because of the dynamic nature of the Internet, any Web addresses or links contained in this book may have changed since publication and may no longer be valid. The views expressed in this work are solely those of the author and do not necessarily reflect the views of the publisher, and the publisher hereby disclaims any responsibility for them.

Any people depicted in stock imagery provided by Thinkstock are models, and such images are being used for illustrative purposes only.

Certain stock imagery © Thinkstock.

ISBN: 978-1-4620-2022-5 (sc)
ISBN: 978-1-4620-2023-2 (hc)
ISBN: 978-1-4620-2024-9 (e)

Printed in the United States of America

iUniverse rev. date: 7/26/2011

# Contents

# Foreword:
## A Remarkable Spirit of Unity & Service

What words can truly convey the tragedy of September 11, 2001? This attack unified the nation, but now, years later, complacency has set in and people are forgetting. We must work together so that these memories and lessons do not fade.

I am the president of the September 11th Families' Association and co-founder of the Tribute WTC Visitor Center. I'm a native of Great Neck, New York, and spent 37 years as a volunteer with the Great Neck Vigilant Fire Department. I also spent 26 years in the Fire Department of New York City, 19 years in Rescue 2 in Brooklyn.

On September 11, 2001, I received a call from my son Jonathan, father of two young children. He explained that a plane had hit the World Trade Center and that his company (Squad 288 FDNY) would be responding. We spoke for a brief moment as they were being dispatched and I told Jonathan to be careful. That was the last time I spoke to my son.

I arrived at the World Trade Center within a half an hour of the collapse of the North Tower. My mission was to find my son and to help search for the thousands of people who were murdered that day. Three months after the attacks, on December 11, 2001, Jonathan's body was recovered. In the tradition of the New York Fire Department, my younger son, Brendon, also a New York City firefighter, and I, along with some men from Squad 288, were able to carry Jonathan out of the site and bury him at home. I then made a commitment to stay and help in the recovery at the World Trade Center site until it was completed six months later.

It would have been easy to harbor feelings of hate and anger after September, but I felt it was more constructive to promote understanding through education. I can't bring my son back, but I can do my best to work toward a more peaceful future for his children—my grandsons. Like many of the personal journeys after September 11 that you will read in this book, my life's mission was changed forever. I have dedicated much of my time and work to remembering September 11 and the lives lost, and to promoting education and cross-cultural understanding. I am able to do this as the board president of the September 11th Families Association and co-founder of the Tribute WTC Visitor Center, located across from the World Trade Center site in New York.

Tribute WTC Visitor Center offers visitors to the World Trade Center site a place where they can connect with people from the September 11th community. Through walking tours, exhibits and programs, the Tribute Center offers "person-to-person history," linking visitors who want to understand and appreciate these historic events with those who experienced them. It is my hope that, through enlightening ourselves and our children, we will truly be able to live in freedom.

We have all been profoundly changed by the attacks of September 11, and many of us in our own way have tried to make tomorrow a little bit better for someone else. The stories shared in this book are illustrations of the strength our nation showed in the aftermath of terrible tragedy. What better way to show the world that the terrorist acts of September 11, 2001, have only strengthened our resolve than to make tomorrow a better place for our children and all the children of the world?

In 2009, September 11, was designated a National Day of Service and Remembrance. After reading the incredible personal experiences in this book and in the spirit of September 11, I ask that you, too, take a moment to think about what you can do to make the future just a little bit better for someone else. You can rekindle the remarkable spirit of unity and service that existed in our nation in the days following the attacks. By reviving this unity, we can honor the victims and pay tribute to the many that rose to service in response.

The personal experiences captured in this book provide a roadmap for our future. I am honored to know many of the contributors and hope that their actions inspire you. It would be such a shame if 20, 50, or 100 years from now, we only had images of death and destruction to define our knowledge of this history. Instead, if we redefine this day as a day of compassion and outreach, we will shape what 9/11/01 means to future generations. Of course we will still have to educate people about what happened on September 11, 2001, and why, but if we couple those facts with service and volunteering, we can promote tolerance and peace.

This September 11, please choose a project to participate in. Help us take back the day and show the strength and power in helping one another.

— Lee Ielpi, President of the September 11th Families' Association

Contributed photo

John Fallon

# Dedication:
## A Very Merry Unbirthday

John Fallon of Wrentham, Massachusetts, unofficially changed his birthday to September 12.

Born on September 11, 1956, after 2001 he simply couldn't celebrate on that day anymore.

"It was out of the question for me to celebrate anything on September 11 out of respect for lives lost and families stolen," says the Boston native. So for the past ten years, he has lit his birthday candles on either the day before or the day after.

"Anything can be taken away in an instant, without warning," he says, so moving his birthday to another day felt like an insignificant sacrifice to make.

The affable and soft-spoken salesman said his rescheduled birthday celebration was a good lesson for his two boys, Jack and Harrison, who have grown up understanding what September 11 meant, even though they were only six and three at the time.

"Every September 11, I now think about what a beautiful day it was in 2001 and I see the image of planes hitting the buildings and the manner in which they crumbled. I think about all of the lives that were lost and all of the survivors, family members, and witnesses, every person on the planet who was changed by these events."

Changing one's birthday is one thing, but changing one's philosophy of life is another. This book is dedicated to everyone who was changed by September 11 — those who have used their gifts to affect the outcome of that day for many. The folks featured in this book have all embraced change for the good. Some changed personal situations and jobs, others found new locations or vocations. Many were called to new careers in the recovery and renewal efforts that took place in New York City and have greatly impacted the healing for so many of those affected.

While John Fallon wasn't in New York City on 9/11, he, like so many others, was affected. In addition to changing his birthday, he greatly altered the way he has approached work since September 11, 2001. The sales manager in the granite industry used to spend a lot of time on the road. "As the years have passed, I travel less and less. I've learned to qualify prospective customers over the phone and even close sales without visiting. It seems as though I may have changed the old model of traveling/selling. As our sons grew up, it became invaluable to me to be with them, to coach them in sports, play catch, and have them know that I was just downstairs in my office."

Today, John plans his business trips to maximize his shorter travel time, just so he can spend more time with his sons and wife, Jill. "I savor every second," he says. "I have very little tolerance for anything that takes time away from my family."

Perhaps his biggest change, he says, was a newfound sensitivity that evolved after 2001. "A change came over a lot of people from what transpired on that day. Many became more tolerant of others, some more polite, some more sensitive, like me."

The avid sports fan says he can't listen to "The Star-Spangled Banner" in stadiums without tearing up as he thinks about those who lost their lives that day: "They never had the chance to give one more hug to their boys or wife. When my youngest son, Harrison, comes down to my office with his baseball glove in hand and asks me to play catch, I have a hard time saying, 'Not right now.' Nothing is more important than family time. Life's too short to say 'Not now.' "

# Acknowledgments

I am grateful to many people who've made my first book more than just a dream. Over the years, I've had numerous dreams for books, but no one idea compelled me the way *Life is Too Short* did.

While I was piling up book ideas in my head, friends and colleagues made sure that this book wouldn't go into the unrealized dream heap.

My heartfelt thanks go first and foremost to all the folks who shared their stories with me. I am forever grateful to the people in these chapters who generously gave of themselves and their time so I could tell their stories.

I also sincerely thank my writing colleagues, especially Regina Clarkin, Sonia Solomonson, Jill Fallon, Gina Chew Holman, Kallie Jurgens, Jerry Zezima, Pat Connelley Pantello, the Rev. Dr. Michael Plekon, and Sharon Cohen for their support.

And to my family, especially my football coach husband, Ken, who always encourages me to "Go big, or go home."

To my friends Joanne Strunck and Grace Kennedy who were there with me on 9/11 and after, and Diane Kittower, my first copy editor and writing comrade, thanks for listening to me on the phone when writer's block and other obstacles presented themselves. To graphic designers Nancy Cataleno and Carolyn Eiseman for their creative spirits, many thanks.

Much gratitude should also go to John Sciblia, the executive director of

Lutheran Disaster Response of New York, who hired me to do the agency's communications and opened the door to my meeting many of the people in this book; and to the Rev. Dr. Stephen Bouman and the Rev. Dr. David Benke, the leaders of the Evangelical Lutheran Church in America and Missouri Synod Lutheran Church in New York City during the 9/11 recovery. They always encouraged me to tell the stories of how God was at work in the aftermath. And to my colleagues at the other 9/11 agencies, especially Ken Curtin, my sincere thanks.

Last but not least, to my furry writing companions — my two Dalmatians, Toby and Summer — who, in spite of their attempts to have me play with them all day, helped me complete my writing. Their paws remain crossed for all those affected by 9/11.

How can I possibly thank my talented photojournalist friend and colleague Dru Nadler who asked me matter-of-factly one day over lunch who was going to take the photos for this book. When I said, "No one. I guess I'll have no photos," she said, "You have to have photos. I'll take them."

And to God, for the gift of writing, perseverance, respect for deadlines, and lots of other things, I am deeply grateful.

# CHAPTER 1

*Introduction:*
*Finding God After September 11, 2001*

Life changed for all of us on September 11, 2001. From having to practically undress at airport check-in lines now, to coming to terms with the fact that Americans are hated in parts of the world, the past ten years have surely been different.

Many have asked over the years where God was on September 11. I've come to conclude that he can be found in the people in this book — those whose lives were changed by the tragedy and who decided to make life a little bit better for themselves and those around them.

The tenth anniversary of 9/11 on September 11, 2011, will undoubtedly be an emotional time. Dr. David Grand, Ph.D., a New York psychologist and trauma counselor who has counseled close to 500 people with issues related to 9/11, says it's important to mark the tenth anniversary for many reasons, first and foremost, to remember the survivors as well as the victims.

"What happens in every disaster," he said, "is that all the attention happens in the weeks and months following the event and as the help recedes, people forget." Commemorating 9/11 is a way to remember the tragedy and to let survivors know that they haven't been forgotten, he says.

We were all affected by 9/11. That's not news. But how some people heard a voice call them through the aftermath is inspiring. Today, many are better able to answer the question "Where was God on 9/11?" as they look back on how life has changed. Many are in vastly different places on this tenth anniversary, either in a new career or a new location, or with a whole new outlook on life. One woman told me that September 12, 2001, was the day she decided that she would work to live, not live to work.

No one learned that lesson better than Chris Conefry, a Wall Street trader who escaped lower Manhattan himself but lost 17 friends as the Towers fell. Today, the native New Yorker and his wife, Erika, are raising their family in a small town near the water in South Carolina. He made the decision to leave New York City's rat race in the years after 9/11. Chris actually provided the inspiration for the title of this book when he told me why he had wanted to move to a place where the pace of life was slow, the weather was warm year-round, and the golfing was spectacular: "I wasn't so much afraid after 9/11, but it was a life-is-too-short sort of thing."

Tom Taylor, a Lutheran pastor on Long Island, needed extra work in the busy and painful days after 9/11 like America needed another terrorist attack.

With an active congregation, a chaplaincy with local fire departments, ecumenical commitments in the community, and a young family, his hands were more than full. Just caring for the emotional and spiritual needs of his congregation after 9/11 was overwhelming. People — even the faithful — were asking, "Where was God?" Words were hard to come by.

But when the Red Cross needed a chaplain at Ground Zero to bless the body parts being picked out of the rubble, Tom immediately got on the train to lower Manhattan. He didn't even think about it. The 9/11 recovery efforts needed help and he had to give of himself.

Everyone did that after 9/11 in New York City. People made the time to help. If ways to respond weren't immediately obvious, people made up their own — like my friend Eileen Smith who was working in the banking industry in Manhattan. She loved to bake and soon had a weekly roster of fire departments that she would visit on her way to work to deliver homemade cookies. A small gesture to show care.

New Yorker Lisa Orloff ran a sweater business. She left her office in the days following 9/11 and headed over to the West Side of Manhattan to the Jacob K. Javits Convention Center where volunteers were spontaneously congregating. She wasn't exactly sure how she could help but she wanted to do something and being with other spontaneous volunteers felt right. She didn't think twice about it.

That's what I did too after 9/11. I was running my communications and marketing business and at the time was very busy. When Lutheran Disaster Response of New York (LDRNY) asked me to help manage its communications program, I didn't hesitate to say yes.

Donations poured into LDRNY after 9/11 to help those in need and the organization had to establish tools and resources to communicate with those affected by the disaster. It needed a Web site, email distribution, newsletters, and collateral materials, all very quickly. Although I was swamped with other work, I made the time for this. It was too important not to. As I think back now, God always made sure that everything on my desk got done, both for LDRNY and all my other clients and, more importantly, that I never lost perspective on the work/life balance.

While I kept my nose in my work a lot back then, I had a lot of energy for it and found it rewarding. I felt like I was helping in the healing efforts and didn't so much mind the late nights I was putting in. I was fulfilled by the people I was meeting, many of whom were affected deeply by 9/11—from the man who lost his son to the woman whose small sewing business in Chinatown was destroyed.

I remember being in awe of the will and the faith of these folks to go forward and I couldn't get them off my mind. I talked with those who had lost loved ones, jobs, homes, and hope. Through LDRNY communications, I shared the stories of Lutheran counselors who worked round-the-clock to help those who were hurting and of the volunteers who hurt too much themselves not to help.

Writing about these courageous people helped me heal from September 11. I was writing the stories of people who lost everything and of those who were giving everything they had to the healing efforts.

No one, however, struck me as deeply as the woman I saw grieving on the family viewing platform that overlooked Ground Zero. The platform was an enclosed 20-foot-by-40-foot makeshift plywood structure that overlooked part of Ground Zero, constructed to allow family members to get as close to their loved ones' remains as they safely could. Handwritten notes pasted on top of each other were scribbled on every inch of the wooden railing that prevented people from falling off the platform. The back wall was a makeshift bulletin board of one-inch-deep layers of photos and notes, along with flowers, teddy bears, and mementos. One Post-It note pasted over a photo read, "Stan, you had a baby girl." Another said, "Happy Birthday." On still another, a woman wrote, "To my beloved husband, I will miss you for the rest of my life."

On April 6, 2002, bishops from the Evangelical Lutheran Church in America from all around the country came to New York City to visit Ground Zero and show solidarity with the New York area pastors. John Scibilia, executive director of LDRNY, had permission to get on the family viewing platform and took the clergy to see Ground Zero up close. I tagged along on their tour of the site to take photos for LDRNY's communications projects. The one photo that I couldn't bring myself to take, however, was the one that I most wanted people to see: an older woman who was sobbing hysterically, now seven months after the tragedy. It was a chilling reminder that September 11 would never end for some.

That woman, in her late 60s I guessed, rocked back and forth on her makeshift seat, perhaps a milk crate, sobbing loudly as she caressed an 8-by-10 photo tacked to the wall of a pretty young woman with long brown hair. Since she was the only family visitor at the platform during my ten-minute visit, it was hard not to notice her. It was like looking at a car wreck. I didn't want to look but couldn't turn away.

Why was she doing this? I wondered. This couldn't be healthy. What ran through my head was, she'll never move on if she keeps this up. After all, it was seven months later. Did she do this every day? Was the pretty young woman her granddaughter?

I knew from talking with the mental health counselors who worked with LDRNY after 9/11 that there was no one way to grieve. We all grieved over September 11 in our own ways. Some made tears public, while others shut

4

down and numbed out. Some turned to booze, while others resorted to anger. Some crawled into bed; others couldn't sleep. The woman at the wall put her grief out there for all to see.

I have thought about this woman at the wall countless times in the ten years since 9/11. While I wondered if she was still grieving in that public way, the courage and faith of countless other victims and family members, responders, and volunteers inspired me. So many turned a horrendous situation into something positive. Out of evil, goodness arose. Many changed their careers, locations, philosophies of life, and their hearts. Many went on to become counselors, disaster response experts, authors, parents, and philanthropists. Some got married when they thought they never would. Others relocated or moved home to family.

Over the past decade, I've kept in touch with some of the survivors and responders that I met after 9/11, several of whom became friends. Amazingly, many are leading new lives today and actually feel blessed to have experienced that horrific tragedy. They say 9/11 helped make them who they are today.

New York trauma counselor Dr. David Grand says some people can move on more easily than others: "Moving on depends on who a person was before the disaster, and how much trauma they carried in their lives." Moving on also depends, he said, on what kind of support system they have and the capacity they have for making meaning out of life events.

Pastor Tom Taylor was so good at counseling first responders at Ground Zero that he went back to school and earned a degree in social work. Today, he has parallel careers as a Lutheran pastor and a mental health counselor.

Lisa Orloff turned her spontaneous volunteer spirit into a full-time career and is now running the World Cares Center in Manhattan, initially a 9/11 volunteer center that later expanded into disaster response training.

Jeremy Bouman, who ran a telecommunications company downtown and supplied cable and phones to many companies in the World Trade Center, decided to leave the hassles of New York City behind after 9/11. He traded the New York City high life for a more stable, safe, and slower pace in the mid-West where he could raise his family and where he now fundraises for a Lutheran college.

These are just three of the amazing stories of courage and faith in those who were changed by 9/11. The common thread that knits their stories together is a sea-change in their thinking. Most concluded after 9/11 that life was too short and decided that they would do what mattered most. They realized that at any moment, life as they knew it could end.

As we mark the tenth anniversary of September 11, let us remember those who didn't get a second chance to make the most out of life and honor those who helped make it better for those who did get that chance.

The Rev. Tom Taylor

# CHAPTER 2

*A Change of Heart: The Rev. Tom Taylor*

*Pastor in the Evangelical Lutheran Church,
Metropolitan New York Synod, and Therapist*

Tom Taylor, a Lutheran pastor for 30 years on Long Island, New York, casually described in graphic detail in dinner conversation how he had blessed a decapitated torso at Ground Zero.

He even described the necklace that was on the torso, down to a minute detail, an engraving that read, "Te amo," "I love you" in Spanish.

As they dove into their seafood dinner, he told his companions about all the gore of blessing body parts and saying prayers in the T-Morgue at Ground Zero, where he had volunteered as a chaplain for five months following September 11.

"How could something like the necklace survive in perfect condition?" he remembered asking. "Just a torso with a necklace hardly even scratched." These words rolled off his tongue as effortlessly as if he were asking to have the breadbasket passed.

While this type of conversation might have been acceptable to a table full of close friends, Tom had only just met his dinner companions several hours earlier. A group of Lutheran pastors had come to New York City to see Ground Zero, talk with fellow clergy about how ministry changed after September 11, and preach at local churches on the upcoming Sunday. It was the spring of 2002 and Tom had already spent five months, from January to May, volunteering at Ground Zero. He fit his chaplain work into the margins of his life as a pastor of Grace Lutheran Church in North Bellmore. The schedule was tough, but he wanted to do his part.

"My wife, Sheryl, nudged me hard under the table and whispered, 'What the hell are you doing?' I was clueless," says Tom. "I had no idea that what I was saying was inappropriate."

In the five months that he had worked at Ground Zero, Tom had become jaded without ever noticing, and immune to the horror he had witnessed. It was now becoming clear that the emotional impact of his work after September 11 was getting to him.

The torso was just one of the horrific things Tom saw in the days after September 11. He had lost all perspective and was in emotional trouble.

He remembers, "When I was first assigned to the morgue, a woman named Sister Grace asked me if I could handle it. Little did I know how it would affect my life."

Tom got the counseling he needed to heal, and this journey would set him on a path towards a new career. His own healing would lead him to new work as a social worker along with being a pastor.

He looks back now, ten years later, in awe at how God opened a door to a new vocation, one that he loves. "I feel very blessed to have worked at Ground Zero and to have met such wonderful people through such a horrible tragedy. Had it not been for 9/11, I wouldn't have met these life-changing people."

Among those life-changers were the mental health counselors whom he sought out for help with his own emotional healing. One psychologist in particular encouraged him to pursue a degree in social work in addition to being a pastor, and to hang out a shingle as a counselor.

Tom had what it took to be a counselor: empathy, good listening skills, patience, and faith. He had spent many years as his local fire department's chaplain in North Bellmore, New York, counseling men who carried dead bodies out of fires and saw plenty of devastation. He was always there for others, never thinking twice about how the tragic stories affected him personally.

But September 11 had brought on his own emotional meltdown, evidenced by his torso story at dinner.

The dinner in New York included Evangelical Lutheran Church pastors from all around the country who had come to the city for a weekend in the spring of 2002 to see Ground Zero. They had come to offer respite to the local pastors who were overwhelmed with mounting post-9/11 pastoral needs — counseling victims' families, preaching forgiveness and hope in the midst of evil, and answering questions about how God could've allowed it.

Arrangements were made for the out-of-town pastors to preach one Sunday so the New York clergy could have a break from church — a sort of "care for the care-givers" weekend, according to Tom.

Tom and several pastors of nearby churches had decided to meet for dinner with the out-of-towners on the Saturday night before church, enjoying a seafood meal over pleasant dinner conversation. The group listened intently as Tom told his stories about being a chaplain at Ground Zero.

Most of his stories were about how he prayed over body parts at the Ground Zero morgue, called the T-morgue, or counseled stunned firemen and police as they brought in horrific remains. Most of Tom's recollections had a thread of inspiration or hope to them.

In one of the more inspirational stories, he told of how a baseball found in the rubble had become a sign of hope for the recovery workers, who had quickly mounted it on a piece of rusty metal twisted to resemble the cross of Jesus. Tom, a baseball fan, was fond of this story: "In all the carnage, you looked for signs of hope and healing. You looked at the 16 acres of nothing at Ground Zero. You looked at death, tragedy, despair, and grief. You looked for anything that could be any sign of good, anything uplifting in any stretch of the imagination."

But when he then went off on a tangent, describing graphic details of body parts, especially of the torso, the dinner guests got quiet.

Ground Zero had clearly gotten to him.

"The chaplains stayed cooped up in the morgue," says Tom. "They didn't want us running around Ground Zero. The job at hand was to bless body parts. When it was convenient or needed, I also could do crisis intervention."

Now, Tom found himself needing his own crisis intervention. He was having what mental health workers called "compassion fatigue."

His wife and several pastor friends suggested he get some counseling.

Counseling would be life-changing for Tom. God led him to a wonderful therapist. Dr. David Grand, one of the world's most renowned trauma counselors who practiced EMDR (eye movement desensitization and reprocessing), a unique type of therapy that quickly helps trauma victims recover and move on. He had an office conveniently down the road from Tom's church. Dr. Grand was a big name in the field of trauma, the kind of trauma that could leave someone emotionally scarred for life.

Dr. Grand practiced trauma therapy and had written the book *EMDR: Emotional Healing at Warp Speed.* When Tom contacted him, he offered to counsel him pro bono as his contribution to the healing at Ground Zero. And, says Tom, "He specifically asked me to sit in on sessions with clients, with their permission, as a spiritual resource. I sat in on over 50 sessions. What a privilege that was."

Even before he went to counseling, Tom had been familiar with Dr. Grand's work. "I vaguely remembered reading an article on Dr. Grand in *Newsday*, about how he did performance improvement work with a golfer. I said to myself, This guy is big time. He isn't going to call me back. He doesn't know me from a hole in the ground, he just wrote a book, he won't have time for me."

But Dr. Grand called back promptly. Tom recalls, "I could tell immediately that David was someone I could trust who had a good soul. I instinctively knew it. He said, 'Why don't you come in. I'll give you a pro bono session. You can see what EMDR is all about.' "

"When I called David, I said that I was overwhelmed with talking to people who needed mental health counseling, especially the firemen, many of whom lost fellow firefighters, and still others who were working at Ground Zero."

Tom quickly learned from Dr. Grand that he was suffering from secondary trauma, feeling the experiences of 9/11 through others. "I was vicariously taking on their trauma," Tom says. All the signs of his stress suddenly made sense — his 40-pound weight gain, the bad eating habits, feelings of nervousness and anger. It was Tom's way of coping with the trauma that he couldn't take time to process because he was too exhausted working at Ground Zero helping others.

Tom was successful with EMDR therapy and quickly got back on his feet emotionally. Knowing that many of the firefighters at his fire station were having trouble getting over September 11, Tom recommended that some of them seek their own counseling: "A guy at a Long Island firehouse, a volunteer at Ground Zero, said to me, 'I'm really having a hard time. I can't function, can't mow the grass, can't do anything, and I'm on medication. I've been to a shrink. Isn't helping.' I said, 'I just met Dr. David Grand. Let's go to him together.' "

Counseling came naturally to Tom. When many of the firefighters were reluctant or scared to go to therapy or thought it wasn't macho, Tom went with them. He says, "Emergency service people, in particular, trust their chaplains. This is a bond that is forever." And Tom, being a good listener and compassionate pastor, had worked with so many firefighters over the years. He knew what made them tick. They felt comfortable and safe with him.

These same qualities gave Tom the emotional fortitude to withstand the grueling work at the morgue. When the Red Cross sent out a call for chaplains, Tom had responded. What the heck, he figured. He was a pastor and could relate to emergency workers. So he went for training in Brooklyn and was assigned to the morgue.

When his work at the morgue ended, he was asked to work at St. Paul's

Chapel, the landmark Episcopal church near Ground Zero. This historic church, where George Washington had worshipped, had become a respite center for recovery workers and a volunteer relief center. This was the church that was recognizable on TV news for the flags, banners, and signs from all over the world that hung outside on the wrought iron fence. It was the place where recovery workers would nap on a cot, get a bowl of hot soup, have their shoulders rubbed, or talk to chaplain Tom and others.

"In the chapel, my role was more laid back than at the morgue. I wore my collar, walked around, interacted with staff and volunteers. It was a ministry of presence," says Tom.

Later, when the chapel opened an exhibit showcasing the memorabilia, letters, notes, and items of support that people had sent from around the world, Tom became a docent.

Life began to normalize for Tom, even though he continued to accompany first responders to counseling with Dr. Grand, reliving the traumas with them. At the same time, he got involved with Lutheran Disaster Response of New York, the disaster response agency of the Lutheran Church. Tom was asked to become the coordinator for Long Island because he knew the area and many victims and families were from there. Tom was also a crucial resource when the agency established its Faithful Response service, a unique faith-based counseling program with Catholic Charities for recovery workers on Long Island.

"I often thought about going back to school for pastoral counseling, using my background in fire service and trauma to help heal people," he remembers.

With David Grand as inspiration and support, Tom enrolled in the social work program at Yeshiva University in Manhattan in 2004, beginning a two-year program for a master's degree.

"When I would sit and watch David do his work, I'd think, Wow, if I could just do half of what he does, what a privilege that could be – what a difference it could make in someone's life."

Managing his studies along with his day job at Grace Lutheran Church — which for a pastor is really a 24/7 job — was hard. But social work was his new calling, and the call was loud. He also had many requests from people asking if they could come for counseling.

"It's important to focus on what God wants me to do — to do more healing in the world, not just through pastoral work but through therapeutic work," says Tom.

"Any way that I can help make my part of the world a little bit better, then maybe I've accomplished something."

With a master's degree in hand, Tom hung out a shingle, working from his church office and meeting with clients when he could fit in the time around pastoral commitments. His first clients were mostly recovery workers and firefighters who were still suffering the emotional after-affects of 9/11, staff and friends from Lutheran Disaster Response of New York, and people from other church-based agencies.

Building a business was slow at first. Being a pastor, Tom didn't have much affinity for business or the acumen for self-marketing. But people kept calling.

From those humble beginnings, he continued to explore different therapies, getting certificates in various types of counseling so he could help more people.

"I'm still seeing one firefighter to talk about 9/11. For some people, the trauma of 9/11 doesn't end."

Through his experiences, Tom says that he has learned to have a grateful heart and "to value each day with more thanks to God for the days that I have."

If any good came out of 9/11, he says, it's the people that he has met who have affected his life, especially Dr. David Grand and the counselors who've influenced his career change. David Grand, once a total stranger offering a random act of kindness, has changed Tom's life.

"I said to myself, I want to sit in David Grand's chair. I'd like to have that kind of feeling, the kind of profound feeling of helping someone. I've enjoyed being a pastor for 30 years, but there was something that was missing. Therapy fills that void.

"September 11 gave me a greater appreciation of human life. It also taught me how much impact not only death and destruction can have, but how much any kind of trauma can impair or immobilize anyone. We all experience trauma differently but this 9/11 level of trauma covered a big geographical area – almost 3,000 people killed from 90 different countries, a major loss of life — and it had such an impact. We won't know exactly how much for years to come."

Jennifer Adams

# CHAPTER 3

## *A Life Change: Jennifer Adams*

### *Chief Executive Officer*
### *September 11 Families' Association*

Before September 11, Jennifer Adams described herself as a "very normal person working in a very normal career."

Up to that point, perhaps the only unique situation the financial consultant had experienced was living through Hurricane Andrew in 1992 as a teen in Miami.

Today Jennifer manages a museum and an almost 4,000-member non-profit organization in New York that supports families who lost loved ones on September 11, 2001.

As the chief executive officer of the September 11 Families' Association, Jennifer has been a leader in family advocacy, communications, and rebuilding after the disaster.

With offices overlooking the World Trade Center site, the organization's mission is to support victims of terrorism through communication, representation, and peer support, and to unite the September 11 community, present evolving issues, and share resources for long-term recovery. It also operates The Tribute

WTC Visitor Center, a museum and visitor center across the street from the World Trade Center site that attracts 500,000 visitors each year.

This unique career change was a surprise in her life. "Before this, I knew nothing about non-profits," she says with a smile. "I thought they were places where you donated clothes."

But after ten years in non-profit work, Jennifer has found a new vocation, one in which she has earned a national reputation. She says, "I never said that this is what I wanted to do. But I was in the right place at the right moment, and it was clearly the right thing to do."

Just prior to September 11, Jennifer was working in investment banking in New York. Having recently relocated to New York City from Miami where she grew up, she was working in the company's World Trade Center office. She was traveling a lot for work and enjoying her twenties in the city. In December of 2000, the company had closed its Manhattan office and Jennifer began consulting, still working from a home base in New York City and traveling more than ever.

Her spontaneous volunteer efforts after the attack quickly thrust her into the September 11 relief efforts and non-profit work.

"Within a day or two after 9/11, I couldn't watch TV anymore and took the initiative to volunteer at Chelsea Piers, the Jacob Javits Center, and at the Ground Zero site for three months," says Jennifer. She felt that she had to do it mostly for her friend Meredith, a financial analyst, who died on September 11.

"Meredith was a good friend who had worked a few floors above me in the World Trade Center. She never came home after 9/11."

Jennifer was working in her day job and volunteering in her spare time, mainly organizing supplies that were being dropped off for the recovery efforts: "Everyone after 9/11 wanted to do something to help. I felt privileged to be in a place to do this. I always thought that anyone in my shoes would have done the same thing."

After the first few weeks, Jennifer found herself volunteering several nights a week, 8 p.m. to 2 a.m., mostly at the supply tent next to the New York Police Department (NYPD) Crime Scene Unit on the corner of West and Liberty streets. The New York Police and Fire Departments and recovery workers were picking up gloves, small tools, ropes, boots, coffee, granola bars, and other items that the Salvation Army provided. Jennifer, who was volunteering at night and working days, was functioning on adrenalin.

She called the tent a "horrible place," but volunteering there was about supporting the people who were doing the recovery work. She says, "We were closed in. It was mentally agonizing. But to be able to hand them a cup of coffee and ask them to talk about their kids as a distraction from what they were doing was the least I could do."

Through her volunteerism, Jennifer met a lot of first responders. Two months after September 11, in November 2001, Jennifer met one of the firemen who initially started the September 11th Widows and Victims Families Association. He had lost many good friends and had started an organization to help families get access to resources and provide information about the recovery.

"He asked me if I would help them," Jennifer recalls. "He realized they needed someone who could help them build the infrastructure of an organization through all of the chaos and emotional instability at that time. He must've had some intuition that I could help in some unique way. Little did I know the journey I was setting out on when I said, 'Sure, I am happy to help.' "

While she didn't immediately start with the association, several months later, in March 2002, she turned down an offer to relocate to Houston with her company. "I didn't want to move from New York," she says.

When it was clear that she would remain in the city, the fireman asked her again to help the organization. Jennifer recalls: "He said, 'In the interim of your employment would you help us?' "

With a small amount of money saved, Jennifer thought she could manage, stay busy, and do this important work during her unemployment, so she rolled up her sleeves and got to work. At first, she said, helping the group was a nice thing to do, but as the organization grew, the work became more important.

Through her work, she met a lot of people who had lost husbands, wives, and children. Among those people were Lee Ielpi who had lost his son, and Marian Fontana whose husband had perished.

Jennifer says, "Lee Ielpi and Marian Fontana were amazing representatives for the families. They were not afraid to speak up and represent the interests of the families — even when it came to difficult and controversial issues. September 11 was so unprecedented that even the most well-intentioned organizations and politicians did not always know what the families needed. Having level-headed family members, who at that point in time could sit down and work with agencies like the Medical Examiner's Office, was helpful in shaping policies and providing assistance, especially when it came to the recovery operations."

As this small group of people associated with the 9/11 Widows and Victims Families Association grew, larger goals emerged. "There were so many unprecedented issues that we felt it was essential to create a communications network for the families to give them a voice." So the grassroots organization, with its humble beginnings, was now able to get on the calendars of the then-Mayor of New York City, Rudy Giuliani, and former New York Governor George Pataki. The group also began working closely with other organizations to identify families who were able to speak about evolving issues.

Jennifer recalls, "We started to connect with other groups and to build a database, and we began communicating directly with thousands of families." The Association united the emerging family groups and began to focus efforts on what a September 11 memorial at the World Trade Center site might look like. The group became the go-to source of information for the families of September 11. "You could see a lack of information," says Jennifer. "NYC was trying to deal with the site, security, the Anthrax scares, and the fire and police departments were running in a million directions. There was a lot that the city was dealing with, in addition to the relief efforts."

By 2003, Jennifer had used up all her savings and needed to earn a salary, so she turned to the leaders of the organization. "I said, 'I've been happy to help you, but I've gone through my entire savings and I have to go back to finance and pay my rent.'" The leadership of the Association told Jennifer that they wanted her to stay. Then something extraordinary happened. Lutheran

Disaster Response of New York, an organization that helped those affected by September 11, agreed to fund Jennifer's salary.

It was around this time that the organization went from a grassroots non-profit to a substantial, cohesive voice in the 9/11 rebuilding efforts. Up to this point, the association was more about representation and communication. Now, with Jennifer as a paid director, it would have a strategic plan to set forth programs as a 501(c)(3), and Jennifer could raise money to keep its efforts funded.

As the Association grew, it began focusing more on a September 11 memorial, recognizing how the families and the Association were shaping history.

"When I was volunteering at the site," Jennifer says, "I never took a picture or thought what I was doing was historic. After I left the site, I regretted not realizing in the moment how historic those activities were."

"It became an important mission for me, especially because of my friend Meredith and the families who needed to have a voice in the process of developing the memorial. We were advocating for the preservation of the site where so many people had died, right on the footprints of the Towers. The families wanted a memorial that would preserve one of the most historic sites in America for generations to come and that would help others understand what happened there."

To help memorialize the history of what happened on that awful day, the September 11 Families Association continued to evolve under Jennifer's direction and opened the Tribute World Trade Center Visitor Center in 2006, a museum and center across the street from Ground Zero."

"The World Trade Center site is now one of the most historic places in America," Jennifer says. "What a shame it would be for kids to visit New York City, walk by the Ground Zero construction site, and never understand what happened there."

She fondly recalls a group of students who had come from Phillipsburg, Kansas, to visit Ground Zero. Showing little interest in the construction site, the group was more interested in their cell phones and NYC souvenirs than in Ground Zero. Lee Ielpi was asked by the group leader to share his personal experience in working in the recovery and about his son who died on 9/11. "When he started to speak, the high school kids got quiet, stopped fidgeting, and started asking questions — it was a memorable moment that those kids would never forget."

It was also the moment that led to Jennifer's idea for the Tribute Center. She recalls: "Lee Ielpi and I were standing at the window, looking at the site as tour bus after tour bus dropped people off. I said to Lee, 'Why don't we try to rent a storefront and have the people we know who were affected by 9/11 share their experience with visitors?' That was the beginning of the Tribute Center. In Lower Manhattan there are hundreds of years of history."

"For many, this is where America began. I realized we were part of that living history and we are here to share it with people. To me it was as important as sitting down in Fraunces Tavern to have a beer with George Washington and asking him what really happened during the American Revolution."

Today, more than two million people have visited the Tribute Center, making it one of the most popular destinations in New York City. Visitors view the exhibits, talk to the volunteers from the 9/11 community: family members, survivors, residents, policemen, firemen, recovery workers, and volunteers who assisted after 9/11. Visitors can talk to and ask questions of those who actually lived through the events of 9/11. It is a healing experience for both the volunteers to talk about their experiences and for the visitors to hear and truly understand the personal side of 9/11.

Ten years after September 11, Jennifer still finds her work fulfilling as the CEO of the September 11 Families' Association and Tribute WTC Visitor Center. Today, she is one of the leading people representing the 9/11 community and manages the Association's 35 employees from offices on Cortlandt Street overlooking Ground Zero.

"Right after 9/11, there was so much emotion and so much happening in the moment, I didn't have time to be reflective here about what we were doing," says Jennifer.

"Now that I look out of the office windows, the granite is being laid for the

World Trade Center memorial pools over the footprints of the Towers, the trees are planted, and it's really nice to see our efforts taking shape."

The families are grateful for her work too: "We get notes from the families that say 'Thank you for not forgetting us.' I'm constantly reminded of why we do what we do."

With her perspective on September 11, Jennifer can now look back and see how she was led to this new career and how the change has transformed her life. "Coming from the finance world, it was all about how much you made and about achieving success. Managing a non-profit and working with people is a totally different measure of success. It is about people and helping them deal every day with the continuing impact of 9/11. I could never have done this without the skills from the business world, but I am certainly happy to have made the transition."

Jennifer recalls how her business skills turned a grassroots families organization into an influential and meaningful voice for victims. "We were really able to have a leadership role in the aftermath and in shaping the future of the site. It was a powerful time for the victims who gained some sense of control in their lives." She now shares her work with other international organizations that represent victims of tragedies.

"Working with the families of 9/11, there is so much grief and emotion tied up in the journey, but also a sense of satisfaction. I can really see how I've used my skills in business to build a 'company' out of our little non-profit. With my business skills, I could build the infrastructure of an organization that could succeed. It's like running any other business, but the reward at the end of the day is in your heart."

She's quick to credit her staff, which gives 150 percent because they all feel a sense of pride in the important work they are doing. "What we all do is very emotional and we have to make sure that we're all doing our jobs well. We're working with people who were traumatized."

The experience has changed Jennifer in ways that she is still discovering. "It's changed my perspective on life — who I am, what my legacy is. It's changed my perspective on the values of life and the significance of the impact I can have on people."

"I've matured a lot, especially in what I value in people and in life. Life is very short. My friend Meredith was only 26 years old. She was at the beginning of her life — her biggest ambition in life at the time was to lose weight."

The Golden Rule has become more important in Jennifer's life, too. Her philosophy? "Treating people the way you want to be treated, taking the time, every day, to listen to people."

How would Jennifer like to be remembered in this world? "I hope that I'm an inspiration to other people. I was a very normal person in a very normal field and I wound up in an extraordinary situation. September 11 was so unprecedented. The circumstances educated me."

"After September 11, I thought a knight on a white horse would ride in and the city would go back to normal again. The world changed. I was forced to embrace that change, and in doing so, I realized that you can change things and make them better."

Besides her career transformation, Jennifer says she is now better at understanding people. "I've grown so much. I now understand the value of forgiving people and what going through a trauma does to you. In a disaster, you put one foot in front of the other and go forward. When you stop, it all comes back to you."

"Through it all, I've learned more about the value of relationships — they're even more important than I thought — and how important it is to pass that on."

"In a huge disaster, even one little thing that you do you can make a difference. I'm amazed that I'm still involved, but it has become my long-term work."

Chris Conefry

# CHAPTER 4

*A Change of Location: Chris Conefry*

### Equities Trader

If there hadn't been a September 11, native New Yorker Christopher Conefry says he probably wouldn't have moved to South Carolina, where he now enjoys a more laid-back lifestyle. Or have left his stressful Wall Street trading job. Or concluded that happiness is more fulfilling than ambition.

Losing 17 close friends on September 11 changed his perspective on what really mattered in his life. Happiness was more important than climbing the ladder.

Conefry, an equities trader who had lived in the New York area his whole life, relocated in 2008 to Beaufort, South Carolina, a quaint historic town on the water south of Charleston. Chris, who was 30 and single in 2001, had often considered escaping the hassles of New York City. "September 11 cemented the deal," he says.

He sold his upscale condo with the skyline view in trendy Hoboken, New Jersey, left his good job downtown, and started anew in a small southern town where the pace of life was, well, not New York's.

Still trading equities, he now works near the ocean. Chris's wife, Erika, and son, Cole, have also switched gears to a slower pace of life.

"If there was any correlation between September 11 and moving south, it was learning to make decisions that would make you happy," he says. "It wasn't a case of me being afraid of being in New York City because of another 9/11, it was more of a life's-too-short decision."

Erika was an easy sell on the move, since she was living in Washington, D.C., on September 11, when the Pentagon was attacked. Having Erika back in his life was a nice surprise, too. The couple had dated in college, had gone their separate ways, and had then reconnected right after September 11.

"New York City was wonderful for the 15 years that I lived there," says Chris, the native Long Islander. He enjoyed the high life, especially hanging out with the young financial crowd on Wall Street. "We played golf, ate at all the nice restaurants, took trips, watched games. It was all fun."

But September 11 changed the game, he says. Suddenly, his colleagues were spending more time with their families. "It wasn't centered on having fun anymore," he says. "I had lived in my own little bubble world. We all had."

Just how much life changed, he says, depended on how affected you were by September 11. For Chris, losing 17 friends, two especially close ones, and dozens of colleagues was a major wake-up call.

Chris was working downtown several blocks from the World Trade Center on September 11. He remembers, "The day was a ten. I remember every detail of the day. I took the ferry to work, which I had been doing for seven years, and walked the six blocks to 390 Greenwich Avenue. I met with a customer named Tommy, who is now my partner, to look at a trading system. Futures were up. The Dow was up. It was a good day.

"A colleague came running in, white as a ghost, and said that a plane had flown into the World Trade Center. At that point, you weren't thinking jet you were thinking maybe a Cessna. Everyone dismissed it as a freak accident, having not seen the burning building yet, and thinking that it was a bad pilot, not a lunatic or a horrible disaster."

As they turned to watch the news coverage on TV, the reality sank in. Chris recalls, "It was an indelible moment. It registered what was happening."

For Chris and the traders at Smith Barney, it was especially shocking, knowing their colleagues at Cantor Fitzgerald — whom they spoke with on the phones hourly — were on the 101st to 105th floors of the towers.

Within five minutes, phones in the trading room began ringing. Chris says, "There were 1,000 of us in the room and everyone was on a phone." Then they were told to leave the building through one door. Before leaving, he made a phone call.

"My parents were in Ireland and the one thing I thought to do was to call their home and leave a message. I said, 'I'm OK, and I'm going to fight to get to Hoboken.' "

Once outside, he realized that buildings were burning and people were dying. Ending up on the West Side Highway, parallel to the Hudson River, he luckily found his good friend Jeff LeVeen whose father was senior sales trader at Cantor Fitzgerald. Jeff's father would be one of the people lost, along with two-thirds of his firm, making Cantor Fitzgerald one of the most tragically affected businesses on September 11.

The two took a minute to figure out what to do and decided to go north. Chris stopped to take $1,000 out of the bank, noticing that gray soot was beginning to cake on his clothes.

Chris ran to the 23rd Street ferry dock and was stunned to find people lining up in an orderly fashion. People, he says, were worrying that they didn't have tickets or cash, since they had left their offices so quickly. "I said, 'This is World War III, don't be worried about tickets. Let's get on this boat and get across.' "

As he calmly walked onto the ferry, he didn't think the scene was horrific — yet. On the ferry, however, a woman who had seen people leaping from the Towers was hysterical. Chris realized that he was one of the lucky ones.

The ferry made the 30-minute Hudson River crossing and brought the passengers to Weehawken, just north of Hoboken where he lived.

As he walked the two miles to his apartment, along the river bank, Chris watched as the two Towers fell. "There was so much smoke, I didn't know if the tops had fallen off the buildings. You worried about them tipping over, not disintegrating like that."

When he got to Hoboken, residents were out in the streets trying to make sense of the confusion. No one wanted to be alone.

In the days that passed, Chris started to realize how on-edge he was. His vibrating cell phone startled him. Awaking to a thunderstorm made him so anxious that he drove to the hospital. "I couldn't calm myself down."

This would be the beginning of his panic attacks, especially when he had to get on a plane. "I wasn't always the greatest flyer, but it was now becoming a problem that I'd have to talk to the flight attendant about."

The panic attacks continued for years after September 11. "It was New Year's 2006 and we went to Scottsdale, Arizona, with ten people. I didn't want to get on the three-hour flight from New York, but I decided to tough it out. The panic attack started right after takeoff. I said, 'Oh my God, I'm stuck on this plane now.' I grabbed Erika and told her to tell the flight attendant that I wanted to get off the plane right now."

It wasn't just the long trips either. Short trips made him anxious too. "In one episode, we flew to Florida and had to rent a car to drive back because I wouldn't get on the plane."

After seeing a cognitive therapist, Chris battled and solved his panic attacks. "When you understand the science behind an attack, then you can deal with it. I now understand that I'm not the best flyer, but I can cope with it. It's not the end of the world."

While he was coping with his panic over flying, he was also feeling guilt about surviving September 11 when so many friends died. He felt even more guilt about not being able to move on. "Everyone seemed to have gotten over it and moved on. Why was I still feeling the effects well into 2003?"

Therapy helped him understand how September 11 would affect his life forever. He was also better able to comfort friends who lost loved ones on that day, especially his friend Jeff LeVeen, who had lost his dad.

Jeff now spends a lot of time visiting Chris in Beaufort, and the two golf enthusiasts spend free time playing at the Secession Golf Club.

In South Carolina, Chris is intentional about making the most out of each and every day. He says, "A lot of it is making sure you laugh every day. Laugh to the point of tears. It really does make a difference."

While still being ambitious, people should not be afraid to take a day off, Chris says. "Don't take anything for granted. No one is immune to tragedy or calamity. Tell people you love them every day. Tell friends how much you enjoy being with them."

In 2002, members of Secession Golf Club in Beaufort started a college scholarship in the name of the late Jeff LeVeen Sr., and Steve Roach, a brother of a friend who also perished on September 11. In conjunction with the golf club, $1 million has now been raised for the LeVeen-Roach Scholarship Fund for local students who might not otherwise have the means to attend college. So far, 25 young men and women have graduated.

While Chris misses some aspects of New York, he says, there are other elements he doesn't miss, which makes him appreciate his change of location even more. "Last time I was up in New York, someone at a stoplight laid on the horn because the car in front wasn't moving fast enough, and it grated on my nerves."

And while September 11 will always be a part of who he is, he takes comfort in a slogan that is close to his heart: Never forget. "This couldn't be more appropriate for what it means," he says. "It would be insulting to forget. Ten years later is way too soon to be apathetic about September 11."

It is a slogan that Chris will have firsthand experience with when explaining its meaning to his toddler son, Cole, when he's old enough to understand.

The Rev. Dr. Willard Ashley

# CHAPTER 5

⌒*w*⌒

## *A Written Change: The Rev. Dr. Willard Ashley*

*Director of Field Education, Associate Professor of Practical Theology,*
*New Brunswick Theological Seminary, New Brunswick, New Jersey*

*Co-Author of* Disaster Spiritual Care: Practical Clergy Responses
to Community, Regional and National Tragedy

The Rev. Dr. Willard Ashley was driving to the doctor's office in Englewood, New Jersey, when the planes struck the World Trade Center. The senior pastor and founder of the Church of Abundant Joy in Jersey City wasn't quite sure what had happened. "I thought maybe a crop duster had hit," he says. But by the time he pulled into the parking lot, the radio news was reporting a terrorist attack.

As a pastor and psychotherapist, he had mixed feelings about whether he should even bother with his doctor's appointment. It all seemed so inconsequential now.

"As the caregiver, I was more worried about the people in the doctor's office," he says. "I wondered if my physician and the staff and patients knew. I felt like I should be the caregiver for the doctor's office."

A caregiver was exactly what Willard was. The nature of his vocation as pastor, psychotherapist, and consultant always put him on the listening end of things. It had been this way ever since he had left his position as assistant buyer for women's hosiery at JCPenney at age 25 to go into the ministry. "I'm a caregiver. My titles are just the different names for the ways I offer care to people."

It wouldn't be until a few years after September 11, 2001, that he would fully recognize the extent of his gifts as a caregiver. Willard would emerge as the face of disaster spiritual care in New York City, helping pastors care for themselves after September 11 and writing the book on care for the caregivers. In 2008, he co-authored *Disaster Spiritual Care: Practical Clergy Responses to Community, Regional and National Tragedy,* the first A-to-Z manual on pastoral care in a disaster.

Pastors, he says, were often at a loss for words on how to explain the evil that had occurred. Working long hours counseling church members and victims' families, he would find that sometimes the needs would be more than he could handle in a 24-hour day. "Pastors were burning out," he says. The term used in the spiritual care world is "compassion fatigue." Most people turned to their pastor after September 11, even before a family doctor or therapist.

Willard would find out firsthand what compassion fatigue meant. In counseling his own church members, working with the Jersey City community — which had been on especially high alert after the 1993 World Trade Center bombers were found there — and providing counseling at The Riverside Church on the upper West Side of Manhattan, he wasn't caring for himself. Hectic days and nights were all added to Sunday services and routine pastoral commitments. He still had to visit people in the hospital, conduct funerals, weddings, and baptisms, and do the everyday work of running a large church.

"Colleagues told me, 'You should take of yourself, but by the way, can you help these 29 people first?' " he laughs. He was exhausted.

"Church members were in survival mode, too," says Willard. "Three or four people worked in the Towers. One went downstairs for coffee and never went back up. Another church member was late to work that day and avoided the disaster." Church members were really nervous, he says. If they didn't work right downtown, many Abundant Joy members still traveled to jobs throughout Manhattan.

Children in the Abundant Joy School had looked out the window in Jersey City and watched the planes hit. They could see the smoke rise from Ground Zero.

"My gut response as the caregiver/psychotherapist was to help these church people. I said to myself, I have to help people process this. We have to tell the happy stories, of those people who got out alive."

For months, Willard met at the church with members and neighbors to tell stories of hope and healing. It was how the people at Abundant Joy were coping and moving forward.

Willard was also consulting with Wall Street firms in the days following 9/11. They hired him to help employees. He remembers, "I was leading small groups of mid-level managers so they could process what had happened. I heard a lot of, 'My colleague jumped out the window,' and 'I made it out of the building, but I heard thuds and I realized what those were, and I don't want to work in NYC any longer.' "

Willard recalls counseling about 600 downtown employees in the first few weeks after September 11. He offered trauma counseling to the employees and consulted with the corporations on what they could expect from their workers following the disaster. In between, he taught at New York Theological Seminary.

Willard's busy days and evenings were filled with people, but his late nights were lonely. He was adjusting to being single after his divorce a few months before 9/11. Living alone for the first time in 22 years, he was trying to make a new life for himself. He recalls, "I would fall asleep at night by watching the lights and smoke of Ground Zero from my New Jersey apartment. I was living on the 48th floor of a luxury high-rise building in Guttenberg. I had a nice downtown view of New York City. I could see clear from 57th Street to the Statue of Liberty. Every day I saw the smoking Towers. I would take out my binoculars for a better view for months, until I fell asleep at night."

If the sights weren't stressful enough, the eerie sounds were frightening. His building was directly in the flight pattern for Newark Airport. "The planes would go right over the building. I was always afraid that one would hit the apartment."

The health problem that he had initially seen the doctor for on September 11 was giving him trouble again. Burdened by compounded stress and exhaustion, he landed in the hospital at the end of September.

"You can't counsel that many people in such a short period of time and not feel it," he says. "I was living on coffee and three hours of sleep. My intellectual side said I was going to crash, but my emotions said keep going. My body made the decision for me."

He spent eight days in the hospital with nothing to do but think. "I contemplated the physical-mental connection of 9/11," says Willard. "I was processing what happened through a few different lenses."

When he was released from the hospital, he tried immediately to return to his hectic pastoral/psychotherapy schedule, but he wasn't healthy enough and soon crashed. "On my first trip back to the city, I was reminded of the fast pace at which Manhattan moved. I relapsed and was back on my back again."

His doctors told him that until he had the strength to keep up with NYC's fast pace, he would have to take a back seat. "My colleagues told me, 'Keep your butt out of NYC,' " he smiles. It took him four months to finally feel good again.

About the same time that he felt ready to return to New York City, a friend at the American Baptist Church asked him to lead a workshop on spiritual care for the clergy. "Pastors were saying, 'We're clueless about what to say to our members. What thematically and theologically should be in the sermon?' " Willard recalls. They wanted to know about the longevity of a disaster and what to expect in the months that followed.

Willard's experience in pastoral psychotherapy and marriage and family counseling made him a perfect choice to lead the workshops. He also knew personally what it was like to crash and burn. "This put me in the disaster spiritual care orbit," he says.

As Willard began his work in disaster spiritual care, the New York faith denominations were trying to organize into one faith-based disaster response group. Each mainline church had been doing what it could to help those affected by September 11, but it began to make sense to consolidate these efforts under the direction of the Council of Churches of the City of New York (CCCNY). New York Disaster Response Interfaith (NYDRI), the early predecessor of New York Disaster Interfaith Services, was gaining traction. NYDRI needed someone to write a grant proposal and turned to Willard: "I was now on the radar screen for disaster spiritual care. I felt all along that God was leading me to this — the long way."

From 2002 to 2007, Willard worked for CCCNY as its first project director of the Care for the Caregivers Interfaith Program in a position funded by the September 11 Fund and the New York Red Cross. He says, "The first thing I did was to look at the Oklahoma City bombing, using that as a model for what we in New York would have to do so that pastors wouldn't burn out and leave." What they learned was that after the Oklahoma City bombing in 1995, many clergy left the ministry. Sixty-six percent of pastors leave the vocation after a disaster, Willard says.

The reason pastors leave, he adds, "is that after a disaster, we get our 15 minutes in the sun and then the phone stops ringing." Pastors often feel they aren't helpful anymore. In addition, he says, after a disaster a congregation will often need a new set of skills in a pastor. "Unless you get retooled, both you and the congregation will get frustrated."

In his new job, Willard was mapping out a retooling program and identifying the fallout from Post Traumatic Stress Disorder, from which many pastors and congregations suffered. He was also orchestrating a program of self-care, inviting clergy members to have regular small group discussions.

Willard told the clergy that it would take about three to five years to get back to normal — back to the ground zero of a church. "By 2005," he says, "things were getting back to normal," something he felt good about. He felt that he had made a good contribution to the spiritual care and healing of the clergy.

As the face of disaster spiritual care in NYC, Willard was now being asked to speak on lessons learned and best practices. When he looked for written materials to hand out at his speaking engagements, none existed. "My friend said, 'Of course it doesn't exist. You didn't write it.' "

As God planned it once again in Willard's life, he would begin to write more than a few handout sheets; he would eventually co-author *Disaster Spiritual Care* with New York Rabbi Stephen Roberts. The rabbi, who Willard knew from his work with Disaster Chaplaincy Services, had a contract to write a book and welcomed co-authorship.

The two started writing the book, a manual for clergy, at the end of 2007 and by 2008 it was published.

Becoming an author is just one of the ways that September 11 transformed him. "For the first six years after the attack I was a single person," he recalls. "I was a workaholic and I learned how to listen in a different way. They teach you how to listen through the psychotherapy process. After coming out of the hospital, I was changed as a caregiver and a clinical psychotherapist. You know how you feel when the chaplain comes to talk to you? But after I was healed, I felt exuberance. God got me through it."

"The disaster made me realize that I was a caregiver. If I look back on my life, I've always been a caregiver."

The disaster also taught him to be more appreciative of his life. "I don't take goodbyes and hellos for granted. When I see someone the next day, I'm happy in a different way. I don't feel it's a guarantee that just because I do the right things all day that I'll come home tonight."

"You eat right, you live right, but life isn't always fair. The disaster allowed me to get greater depth into myself. I was always empathetic, but this added greater depth to that."

Willard also remarried.

Where is God leading him next? More consulting, teaching theology, and being grateful to God for his many blessings.

"God cares for me, and so I care about people."

Lisa Orloff

# CHAPTER 6

*A Change of Direction: Lisa Orloff*

Executive Director of the World Cares Center

A career switch from selling a fashion line under her name to becoming a disaster response expert wasn't in Lisa Orloff's long- or short-term plans.

Before September 11, 2001, she made sweaters. Not knitting a few rows as a hobby in front of the TV at night, but designing, producing, importing, and selling a fashion line under the name of Lisa O.

Working from her office on 14th Street in Greenwich Village, not far from the World Trade Center, this young fashion designer had a good life. In addition to running Lisa O, over the years she had shown factory workers in developing countries different methods of sewing and taught them about manufacturing quality control.

"I had good experience working with diverse communities," Lisa says. Perhaps it was that experience or her skills as an entrepreneur that helped her emerge as a leader in the volunteer efforts following September 11.

Today she is the executive director of the World Cares Center, a New York City organization that began after the World Trade Center disaster. Lisa's post-9/11 dream, which started as September Space, has provided disaster preparedness, response, and resilient recovery services and training to more than 45,000 people in twenty-four states since its humble beginnings at Ground Zero.

Drastically different from her career in fashion, her new vocation emerged because Lisa instinctively went to the Jacob K. Javits Center on Manhattan's West Side to volunteer in any way she could after September 11. The Javits Center, a large convention center on the Hudson River, was the makeshift focal point for organizing volunteers. Their effort became known as the Spontaneous Unaffiliated Community Volunteers, and it has served as a model for volunteer response in other disasters.

For weeks during the 9/11 rescue, recovery, and cleanup, thousands of volunteers from the tri-state area organized the supplies that streamed into the city, arranged for deliveries, managed logistics, and otherwise lent a hand where needed. The spontaneous volunteers were often seen on TV news standing on the West Side Highway waving and holding signs to cheer on the responders and recovery workers who traveled by the Javits Center to Ground Zero each day.

"I initially went down to St. Vincent's Hospital to try to donate blood," she says. "I walked around Chelsea Piers looking for a way to help out and volunteer and they sent me to the Javits Center because they needed help up there." She ended up becoming one of the organizers of both people and supplies in the massive volunteer effort.

"At the Javits Center, I saw two people sitting at a 3-foot-by-3-foot folding card table handing out fliers about where to go to donate blood."

She proactively took the fliers and started handing them out to people coming to the Javits Center. She began helping the Salvation Army organize its efforts to feed the massive numbers of volunteers being deployed to Ground Zero, doing whatever tasks she could.

"A doctor who was helping to organize supplies saw me assisting the Salvation Army and asked me to help him," says Lisa. "So I began organizing medical supplies that were coming to the Javits Center — medication, gloves, masks, you name it." From there, the coordinating doctor and others recognized her as a leader. Soon they brought volunteers to her to manage. She began matching up people with tasks such as sorting through medications and storing supplies.

At one point she was asked to accompany the medical teams to Ground Zero and work in one of the triage units. There she assisted doctors in giving eyewashes to the rescue workers.

"It was a surreal experience," she says. "I never did anything like that before. New York City is a very vibrant, alive, and noisy place, with lots of things going on at once. That evening was like walking in the middle of a snowstorm. Noises were muffled. It was like you were in a snow globe covered with ash."

Quickly gaining a reputation as a go-to person for volunteers, Lisa began tracking down needed supplies. She went to the triage sites at Ground Zero and asked the workers what was needed. Handing out her name and number, she mapped out where groups where working and what they needed.

When the Army National Guard arrived at the Javits Center, a sergeant needed a prescription filled and turned to her for help. It was delivered to him within the hour. "He was surprised at how fast I could do this," she remembers. "He was so grateful that he said to me, 'Anything you guys need, just ask.' So I said, 'I need a truck and two drivers.' He said, 'Give me 20 minutes,' and I had them."

Her days soon were filled with loading up the truck at the Javits Center, organizing volunteers, and securing or delivering the needed supplies. "One of the first groups I met at Ground Zero was an EMS group in Queens," she says. "One of the things they needed was a defibrillator, and when I got it delivered to them, they were shocked."

As Lisa worked with the spontaneous volunteers, she realized that a more organized effort was needed. So she teamed up with another volunteer, Polly Dufresne, and the two collectively organized a group called NYCan. They were now managing close to 300 volunteers.

While the NYCan network worked well, Lisa had a broader vision. She dreamed of a community center for volunteers and rescue workers where programs could help the responders heal and move on. September Space was born.

"I had seen how disaster response was taking its toll on the responder community as a whole. I wanted to do something for them," she says.

As a volunteer leader, Lisa was introduced to the response teams at the Federal Emergency Management Agency and its voluntary agency liaison, who suggested she connect with Voluntary Organizations Active in Disaster (VOAD). Through VOAD, she was introduced to Lutheran Disaster Response of New York (LDRNY), the agency that worked with the Lutheran Church to help those affected by 9/11. Along with Thrivent Financial, a financial services organization for Lutherans, LDRNY offered to fund Lisa's dream of September Space.

"The space was donated to us, and LDRNY and Thrivent gave us $200,000 to get started," she said. It was a dream come true.

With office space on 8th Avenue donated by Newmark Realty, she began overseeing renovation of the community center. She asked others for help, getting pro bono construction help to renovate office space into a community center.

In 2002, the September Space project was complete and the organization was incorporated as World Cares Center, receiving its official nonprofit status. At first, the center offered programs such as art therapy, support groups, and yoga for responders and their families. Years later, it emerged as a collaborative organization that provided grassroots support to local community members as resilient first responders through other disasters, including Hurricane Katrina and the earthquake in Haiti.

Lisa wrote a training manual and developed learning modules on how disaster agencies could manage spontaneous volunteers. Her manual, "Leading and Managing Spontaneous Unaffiliated Community Volunteers," has been delivered to 24 states. She also began writing "Grassroots Readiness and Response," a manual for the general public.

During the height of the September 11 recovery effort, World Cares Center had 15 employees and two September Space community centers in Manhattan.

With funding decreases in New York City over the years, Lisa was forced to make cuts to her 9/11 programming. Today, the Center has six employees and 15 facilitators and focuses mostly on fostering sustainable, locally led disaster preparedness, response, and recovery initiatives.

"We work with a lot of communities," Lisa says. "It's all about teaching."

Lisa went to the Gulf Coast in 2005 after Hurricane Katrina and to Haiti in 2010 when the island was devastated by an earthquake.

"We've gone through huge changes and learning curves," she notes. "That is the nature of what we do. We want to challenge ourselves and do the best that we can. It took us a while to get there, but we're there. We are acknowledged by the best as the subject matter experts in spontaneous volunteer management and community engagement."

The fact that September 11 brought out her volunteer spirit in a big way was no surprise. "As a kid, I was always rooting for the underdog and trying to help out. It really is who I always was."

But the stakes were a lot higher after September 11. "Dealing with emotionally traumatized individuals was very hard," she says.

While she is content in her new career, she misses the creative time she had when she ran Lisa O, her sweater company. "I have very little time for taking a few hours and doing something that is visually or tactilely enjoyable. I enjoyed that right-brain time," Lisa says with a smile.

But her career change has brought a new perspective on life: "I have a more positive view of people. I look at the potential that they have to do good. I look at people and see how they can make a difference. I'm interested in learning about people and their skills and how they can help what we're doing."

She plans to do something memorable on the tenth anniversary of September 11. She wants to spend quality time with some of the people with whom she volunteered. "Everyone sees me now as the executive director of the World Cares Center, but I'm a volunteer just like everyone else."

She also welcomes help at the Center, which will always be ready to guide communities to respond to disaster.

"Disaster response takes an ecosystem of small and large agencies working together. It's not about any one agency. It's about all entities working together. We will always need each other."

Ann Mahoney Kadar

# CHAPTER 7

*A Dramatic Change: Ann Mahoney Kadar*

*Drama Department Director*

*Asheville Arts Center*

From her balcony in Brooklyn, Ann Mahoney Kadar watched the Towers collapse and burn. Ann, then 23, awoke on the morning of September 11 to a cacophony of ambulances, fire trucks, and police sirens. "I looked at my roommate and said, 'This is the end of the world.' "

The neophyte New Yorker should've been looking at her exciting new home through the eyes of someone who had just moved to New York to make it big on Broadway. Instead, dust, debris, and smoke clouded the view. As an aspiring actress, she was used to acting out emotions; but this time, the fear was all too real.

September 11 wouldn't be the first disaster she would experience. When acting opportunities in New York City dried up following September 11, the New Orleans native moved home in 2003, only to have her house flooded in Hurricane Katrina.

"In the past ten years," says Ann, now 33 and living in Asheville, North Carolina, "the best things and the worst things in life have happened to me."

While losing her dream career in New York City and then her home in New Orleans both weighed heavily on the "worst" side, meeting her husband in a NYC subway in 2003 and having her son Rumsey in 2007 were on the "best." "It's certainly been balanced," she smiles. Today, she is the drama department director at the Asheville Arts Center in Asheville, North Carolina.

On September 11, it was ironic that Ann felt that the world was ending. She had just moved to New York City a month before to start a new life, a new beginning. With a master's degree in acting from the University of Connecticut in Storrs, she was ready to take on Broadway, or any acting role for that matter. "I had a picture in my head of what life would be like. I was going to do the Broadway thing and be a big actress," she says.

In only a month, she had made progress breaking into the very competitive NYC acting scene. But all that groundwork came to a grinding halt after September 11. She remembers, "Doors just started slamming shut."

With Broadway closed down for weeks and New York in turmoil, Ann's thoughts were no longer set on acting but rather on survival. "All I wanted to do was be home with family in New Orleans. I began to reevaluate my life."

At the time, she attended a Lutheran church in Brooklyn, and like all churches after September 11, the congregation collected money for the relief efforts. "We wanted to donate the money to the Red Cross," she says, "but we couldn't read the name on the poster because it was covered in red tape, so someone said, 'Why don't you donate it to Lutheran Disaster Response of New York.' "

Lutheran Disaster Response of New York (LDRNY) was the September 11 response organization of the Evangelical Lutheran Church in America and the Lutheran Church, Missouri Synod. As a leading faith-based response organization, LDRNY had collected more than $9 million in donations for those affected by September 11.

Ann contacted the organization and someone came to Brooklyn to pick up the money her church had collected. She recalls, "The woman, Lena, asked me how I was doing. She suggested that if I needed work, I could contact Chris Connell who worked for Lutheran Social Services of New York."

In conjunction with LDRNY, the agency had started Project LIFE (for

Lutheran Initiative for Enrichment), a case management program for people affected by September 11, and needed case workers, administrative assistants, and other staffers. "I talked to Chris and we immediately got along. I guess she saw something in me," laughs Ann.

Ann became the Project LIFE secretary and in short order got promoted to the chair of the Unmet Needs Roundtable, a place where victims of September 11 could go to get help when they exhausted all other financial assistance. She remembers, "I was matching up social workers with donors, that's what I was doing. I was doing good and doing it well.

"I was making money, but I wasn't fulfilled creatively. I started to feel angry towards the people who were seeking financial assistance, and I knew this job wasn't the right thing for me anymore. I found myself thinking, when I heard the stories, yeah right. I had gotten cynical. While I loved the job and the people of Project LIFE, it wasn't what I wanted to do."

Ann had not been able to shake the fear she had felt on September 11. "I was afraid a lot of the time, and I lived on high alert about what could happen. I got tired of feeling that way."

"It became clear to me that nothing I was doing career-wise would take care of me like family." She wanted to go home.

Wanting to have children of her own and not raise them in New York, in 2003 she convinced her husband, Danny, a record producer whom she had met after September 11 on the 2$^{nd}$ Avenue stop of the F train, to move to New Orleans. "The job possibilities were good, and the film and TV businesses there were booming," she says.

They bought a small house in the best neighborhood they could find, and Ann was enjoying having her parents and younger brother nearby.

For two years, life was good again. Ann established the acting career that she had left in New York, and she began to shake the fear she had felt since September 11. "It was a great move for me. Everything was great. I was actively teaching and acting in plays."

Then Katrina hit in 2005. Ann and Danny's Lakeview neighborhood — only a quarter-mile from Lake Pontchartrain and the 17th Street levy breach — was under water. Recalling the devastation, Ann says, "We lost our house. It was under seven feet of water. It didn't drain for two and a half months.

"We evacuated with suitcases, with three days of clothes and our cat. We left everything else, including cars, and we all went as a family to northern Louisiana." They lived out of three hotel rooms for weeks.

When they were able to return to their home, they knew they couldn't live there. Ann found herself once again not knowing what the future would hold.

She says, "I still wanted to live in New Orleans, and my husband wanted to go back to New York. I sure didn't want to return to the city. I was adamant on that. I knew it would never be the same."

So they agreed to relocate to Asheville, North Carolina, where they have spent the past few years making a new life ... again.

Ann is now teaching acting classes and directing plays at the Asheville Arts Center and enjoying raising her son. She is writing scripts and looking for ways to get back into acting. Her husband is thinking about going back to school to get a master's in audiology.

Nevertheless, she says September 11 transformed her in ways that she has yet to know. "Since Katrina," she says, "it has been a struggle." But she looks back on her young life and knows that these hardships have shaped who she is.

"You put things in perspective," she says. "You come to grips with the fact that you are going to die some day. And so you think about what you really need and want."

"The thoughts only come to you when you're ready. It's something that you have to come to by yourself."

Contributed photo

Jeremy Bouman

# CHAPTER 8

*A Job Change: Jeremy Bouman*

*Director of Corporate and Foundation Relations*
*Creighton University*

After September 11, Jeremy Bouman, 35, saw his wildly successful downtown telecommunications business crash. A business that once had 15 employees working on Broadway had dwindled down to just himself and his partner making do from a tiny office in New Jersey.

"I lost my business in 9/11," says Jeremy. The once booming firm that sold data products, including circuits and equipment for wide-area networks and high-speed Internet, limped along like so many businesses in the beleaguered Wall Street area after September 11. By spring 2002, it ran out of steam.

After closing the business just five blocks from Ground Zero, Jeremy took stock of his life. Living in the fast lane seemed all about the money and that wasn't who he was. September 11 forced him to rethink, regroup, and do a U-turn.

He says, "September 11 focused me on thinking about how I would spend my time on earth — how I would contribute to the greater good. Not just selling Internet connections for money. If I hadn't gotten out of the business, I wonder what I would've become."

But Jeremy wasn't always so enlightened. As a pastor's kid, he saw the money, the instant success, the New York life as new and exciting, and he relished every minute.

He was an agent for corporate giant Nynex/Bell Atlantic, a firm that provided services for many companies in the World Trade Center. As the digital revolution took hold, the telecommunications business was growing. "We had more copper cable below 14th Street in Manhattan than in all of Africa," he laughs.

That all changed on September 11. He recalls, "By December 2001, the business was hemorrhaging. We had laid people off and were losing customers. Commission checks from the phone company were slowing down.

"Our office landlord, a friend who had kept us on as long as he could, told us to find other office space. So we opened a small office in Hoboken, New Jersey." The new space was a far cry from the upscale office he had had in downtown Manhattan.

After buying the business in 1998, Jeremy and his partner had ridden the wave up and were now being pummeled as it crashed down.

"It had been a fun time," he recalls. "We were young guys and New York was booming. It was all new to me and exciting. We were 24, 25 years old, wearing jeans to work, and running big companies. It was like the wild, wild West."

With $1.5 million in sales, Jeremy had investors interested in the business. He was living on the water in Jersey City, money was free flowing, and so was the good life. Partying in Manhattan after work was the norm. "Customers would call their sultans from our office, companies were renting out huge boats for wild parties, and people were throwing cash around."

When business tanked, Jeremy moved to Hoboken in December 2001. While dealing with a struggling business and the reality that it would likely have to close, he started to reevaluate what he wanted to do with this life.

The fact was, he didn't like the person he had become. "I was focused on making money and didn't have the best priorities. I was a greedy kid," he recalls. "We were earning good money, running around the city, and I thought there had to be more meaning to how I spend my time. "

In particular, he thought about all the friends and colleagues who had died on September 11. They would never get a second chance. Jeremy wanted to recreate himself. "There was a humanity that stuck around after September 11, and I wanted to do something more with my life."

When a job opened up in fundraising with Lutheran Social Services of New York, in the Lutheran Church where his father was a bishop, he jumped at it. He started a new career in development, something that he felt helped humanity, and he loved it. "The same excitement I felt when I closed a sale in my business I got when I had a check handed to me. I felt better about myself and my own place in the world. I felt that I was now contributing to more than myself."

The bachelor Jeremy also met Sarah Goringe, the executive assistant to the president of Lutheran Social Services. She was living in Portland, Oregon, and every now and then would come to New York for a meeting. They met in July 2002, dated cross-country, and married in 2005. Sophie was born in 2007 and Luke arrived in 2011.

Jeremy moved on from the social services agency and took another fundraising job with the Lutheran Church in the Delaware-Maryland area. From there, he was offered the position of vice president for institutional advancement at Dana College in Omaha, Nebraska, and today serves as the director of corporate and foundation relations at Creighton University in Omaha.

While he misses New York City where he spent most of his life, he enjoys his new vocation. "I still miss the endless ideas and personalities in New York," he laughs.

"I don't know how I dealt with September 11. To this day, I can't watch anything about it. I can't read anything about it. I wonder whether I stayed away from New York because I chose not to deal with it. I try to wrap my head around the things I saw or smelled, the bodies, the pain. In the end, I know I needed to get distance from it."

He does admit that the heartland of America is a safer place to raise a family, and provides a nice way of life. And the threat of another September 11 doesn't feel as great.

"Since September 11, I'm much more focused now and a more mature person," Jeremy says. "I discovered who I was and found a career and meaning for my own life. I wonder if I would have come to that if 9/11 hadn't happened? I probably would've stayed in the business, tried to get absorbed by a bigger company, had a quick pay-day, and used the money to open a bar or do something less meaningful."

Mikki Baloy Davis

# CHAPTER 9

## A Healing Change: Mikki Baloy Davis

### Shamanic Healer

For Mikki Baloy Davis, 32, the long road to emotional healing from September 11 came during her efforts to help others during the recovery and aftermath.

It was after she had healed from what she had witnessed that she realized she was destined to be a healer in the ancient sense.

Learning a new craft as a shaman, or spiritual healer, allowed her to move on from the disaster, which she not only lived through but worked through with victims at Ground Zero for years afterward.

The best part of studying with a shaman, she says, was learning about resiliency and what makes people bounce back from tragedy: "I now have a much deeper understanding of what it means to heal. I understand resiliency. I went through it myself after September 11, and saw people doing it, but never understood why some people moved on and others were stuck."

She says the Number 1 lesson learned from September 11 is that healing is always possible even in the midst of abject horror. "There is always a resource, always a hand, always something that you can get when you need it."

Transitioning to a healing profession was a natural for Mikki, who was drawn to the practice even as a kid. "I remember being really tiny and emptying my piggy bank to give money to poor people. I felt compelled to give my 37 cents to those in need."

"What makes people start to heal is their willingness to stand face to face with what scares them; to explore the dark stuff. Just because I went to work after September 11 didn't mean I wasn't traumatized. In fact, the person sucking his thumb in the corner after September 11 might have had the most honest reaction."

When she was able to move on from September 11, Mikki found that the door opened to many other life changes too. She became Buddhist, a practice she began studying in college, found love, got married, left Brooklyn for the suburbs, and changed careers.

Today, she runs Pamo Healing, a wellness practice in Pleasantville, New York, using alternative therapy approaches such as ancient Peruvian shamanic techniques, Reiki, Eastern philosophy, creative expression, and contemporary science. She is gratified by helping people better understand that the mind, body, and spirit are ultimately one, and that the power to heal is within. She works with people who have acute or chronic injuries, illnesses, depression, confusion, stress, phobias, and those who are feeling stuck. Pamo means "warrior" in Tibetan.

"There are great gifts to be had in being of service to other people," she says. "It is not all altruism and being holy, holy. Healing can be a reciprocal partnership."

But Mikki didn't always want to be a healer. She wanted to be an actress. That's the dream that landed her in New York City right before September 11, when she came to the city after graduation from Hartwick College in upstate New York for an audition. "I had $400 in my pocket and a job at a bookstore," she recalls. She was living with a friend in Brooklyn and took a better-paying temp job while she planned to pursue her acting career.

On September 11, she was working downtown in the temp job. After the planes hit, the office was remarkably calm. "We felt the building shake and an elevator hit the shaft, but we had no idea what had happened. We didn't know enough to panic," says Mikki. With no TV in the office, and the phone lines down, she looked out the windows and all she saw was pitch black. The staff wasn't sure what to do, she says. People remained in the building for several hours, unsure that it was safe to leave. "All I remember is seeing the falling paper," she says. Ironically, it looked much like the confetti thrown down during the parade when the New York Yankees win the World Series.

When it became clear that they should evacuate, Mikki loaded her pockets with Band-Aids and a granola bar — items that were nearby and made sense at the time — and headed for the staircase. As she flew down the long staircase, employees from a textile company several floors down handed out fabric swatches so people could cover their mouths.

"They were shoving swatches of fabric under doors to keep the smoke out."

With a swatch covering her mouth, Mikki was glad to have it when she got outside and saw light. With inches of dust already covering everything, she began to realize that what was happening was huge.

As she rushed up Pearl Street, she passed what she remembers now as surreal sights: a pair of shoes left on the street, an abandoned donut cart, a taxi cab with the door wide open. She got a dial tone on her cell phone and called a friend working uptown. The two decided to meet in the East Village and walk the 35 blocks to the Brooklyn Bridge to head home. By the time she got to the bridge later that day, another building at Ground Zero had fallen.

She recalled meeting friends the next day and walking aimlessly around the streets of Brooklyn. "We didn't know what to do with ourselves," she says. "We would bake cookies and hand them out to the firemen and police, just to do something. We just stood at the waterfront and stared at the site of the World Trade Center."

A week later, she returned to work, and found a new job four months later at a day-trading firm on Wall Street. She worked there for about a year and became a victim of the failing downtown economy following September 11. She lost her job and was out of work for about three months.

After weeks of watching too much TV and feeling lifeless and depressed, she learned from a friend about an administrative job with a disaster relief fund, Lutheran Disaster Response of New York, for those affected by September 11. Her job was initially to support the director, and when he left she assumed a leadership role, staying in the position for six years until it sunsetted, the term used for "closing down" in the disaster response world.

From offices at Ground Zero, Mikki had day-to-day contact with those affected by September 11. Sharing an office with the New York Disaster Interfaith Service, she was part of the rebuilding planning that went on after September 11. FEMA and other disaster relief agencies were often in the office for meetings. She also worked closely with the September 11 Families' Association that initially shared office space with her agency.

Working so closely with victims and families, Mikki had the wherewithal to understand that she needed her own counseling to manage the stress. This counseling would lay the groundwork to start her own healing business years later.

"The more I resolved my own stuff, the deeper the well I could source to help other people heal," she says. "Had I not forced myself into therapy early, I wouldn't have been able to get my act together enough to be there for others."

While overlooking Ground Zero from panoramic windows in her office every day, Mikki experienced several transformational moments. Perhaps the most significant, she says, was deepening her study of Buddhism. "I was a generic lapsed Catholic, not going to church but studying religion in college and discovering Eastern philosophy and Buddhism. When I moved to NYC, I meditated more and started going to Buddist classes and retreats."

"I wanted a sense of community and I wanted a set of tools to help me deal with what I was going through. I was living in the city, battling depression, and the thought of going to church and praying to something didn't seem tangible to me."

For one vacation, she went on a trip to Nepal and embraced Eastern philosophy. Soon after, she transitioned to Buddhism.

Having no luck with the NYC dating scene, she had temporarily sworn off dating, although she had had a few serious relationships. She hadn't found Mr. Right and was fed up with looking. "I always knew at some point that I wanted to wake up with my best friend, but my frustration with dating was that I hadn't found him yet.

"I decided to travel instead of dating," she laughs.

As she was about to pull down her dating profile from an online dating service, she caught the interest of music teacher Russ Davis. "I said to myself, I'll give it one dinner, just one." But after three dates, Mikki and Russ knew they had found their soul mates. In May 2009, they married and Mikki moved from Brooklyn to the suburbs of Westchester County.

In addition to a new relationship and a new home, Mikki was in several other new situations. She was jobless after the disaster response agency closed in 2009. She was still interested in being an actress, and took time after her job ended to pursue her love of acting.

She went from audition to audition, always waiting for the next casting call. When she wasn't having new headshots made, she spent her time worrying about when the next audition would come. She remembers, "I was just miserable. I loved acting, but hated the business side of things. I was sick of walking around with my fingers crossed all the time."

She decided to give up on acting and look for another vocation. Feeling lost, she went to a yoga retreat center in the Berkshire Mountains of Massachusetts and met a shaman who became her teacher. She began to study shamanism and planned her new vocation as a healer.

"My working at the disaster response agency was my way of being a healer after September 11 in the only way that I knew how. But my first practice in what I learned from the shaman was completely electric. I felt so plugged in.

"I had always thought, I'm an actress, I'm an actress. I thought I would have a day job that would satisfy me, and I'd work as an actress at night. But now that's all flipped. It changed when I realized that I was always a healer."

Mikki has September 11, among other events, to thank for that.

Photo by Dru Nadler

KellyAnn Lynch

Contributed photo

Shannon Hickey

# CHAPTER 10

## A Change for Mychal:
## KellyAnn Lynch & Shannon Hickey

### Founders of Mychal's Message

Every year since she was a baby, Shannon Hickey would have a special party in January to celebrate her life. Not a birthday party, but a celebration of the new life she was given with a liver transplant on January 29, 1991, at seven months old.

As Shannon got older and remained healthy, her Landisville, Pennsylvania, family would invite their friends to Shannon's annual party and the children would bring presents. It was a fun celebration of the gift of life Shannon had been given, said mom KellyAnn Lynch.

But after September 11, the party took on new meaning for Shannon, who at 11 turned the occasion into an opportunity to help the less fortunate. Her inspiration was a Franciscan priest who perished helping firefighters in the World Trade Center, Father Mychal Judge.

"Mom, can we have the party this year?" Shannon asked in January 2002. Mom replied, "I don't know, honey. It's a sad time for a lot of people."

Even in January 2002, KellyAnn and her family were still feeling the effects of the September 11 attack particularly deeply. They had lost their pastor and friend, Father Mychal Judge, the Franciscan priest and New York Fire Department chaplain thought to be among the first responders to die on that day.

"We were all mourning Father Mychal," says KellyAnn. "Especially my dad who was an altar boy for him at a church in East Rutherford, New Jersey, in the 1960s. I just didn't know how we would do a party for Shannon when we all were still grieving. Especially without Father Mychal there. He would always come over to the house after Mass when I was growing up, to visit with the family. He was a family friend to all of us."

Then Shannon approached her mom with an idea. She asked, "What if, instead of bringing presents to me, I ask my friends to bring socks to the party, socks that could be donated to the needy?"

Mom agreed and the party was held. Eventually, 1,500 pairs of socks were collected as word got around about the teen's philanthropic project. So began Mychal's Message, a non-profit organization dedicated to the memory of Father Mychal, a well loved friar known for a life of service to others.

Shannon, KellyAnn, and KellyAnn's mother, Sharon Hickey, are the co-founders of Mychal's Message, which today estimates donating more than 300,000 new items since its founding in 2002.

September 11 was significant for the Lynch and Hickey families. "We're doing things today that we never would've done without 9/11," says KellyAnn, the mother of four. Mychal's death taught her how to live.

She began her lifelong mission: to let a generation of children who might not have known who Mychal was hear his message of living a life of helping others.

Says KellyAnn, "You realize what's important. You realize what matters. Wouldn't we want to live our last day on earth helping others like Mychal did? That's the way I want to go to heaven. When I've sacrificed and loved and served, I can be welcomed in his sacrificial love."

Today, in addition to running Mychal's Message with her daughter and mother, KellyAnn goes to parochial elementary schools and church groups teaching about service to others. She reads *"He Said Yes,"* a children's book she wrote about Father Mychal. Both jobs are a big change from her earlier career as a legal secretary.

"I thought that it was about time for me to think about going back to work. After Mychal died, I didn't want to go back and work in a law office, I wanted to work for God. I didn't feel I could make a difference in a law office. I wanted to do something more."

KellyAnn wanted to teach schoolchildren what was learned by Father Mychal's death. "We learned so much from his life. In his death we continue to move forward, and his spirit lives on. He died doing what he loved. I've learned so much since his death. Every year since 9/11 I learn a little more. Mostly about an openness and a non-judgmental way of loving everyone."

After September 11, KellyAnn became a Secular Franciscan in a branch of the Order of Friars Minor, or the Franciscans, for secular ministry. "Right after Mychal died, I made the phone call to become a Secular Franciscan," she says. "I dialed 1-800-Francis. I said, 'We lost Father Mychal. What can we do?' " KellyAnn was professed in the lay ministry in 2009.

"After Father Mychal died," she recalls, "one of the feelings I had was that his life — his legacy — was too important to die with him. It needed to be shared. I often thought about how to get his message out there." She started with a children's book.

KellyAnn was in weekday Mass when she got the idea for *He Said Yes*. "All I could hear in my mind and my heart was 'He said Yes. He said Yes.' I was barely out of the parking lot and I said to my mother, 'What do you think? I've got a great idea. An illustration in the book shows two doves in place of the Twin Towers.' This was something orchestrated by God." Her book was published in 2007.

As KellyAnn teaches children about a life of service today, Shannon is studying communications and broadcasting at Millersville University in Millersville, Pennsylvania.

When she was in high school, Shannon didn't think she was doing enough to help the world by only collecting socks and running Mychal's Message. She started the Home Sweet Home project, a high school program that helped raise awareness among teenagers about homelessness. This offshoot of Mychal's Message asks teens to sleep outside in cardboard boxes to learn what it's like to be homeless. "We had to continue walking in Mychal's footsteps," she says.

Projects like these earned Shannon honors with local, community, national, and international awards, including the Prudential Spirit of Community Award in 2005 and the Sertoma Service to Mankind Award in 2008. She was also recognized by President George Bush in 2004, 2007, and 2008, and was featured on the NBC Today Show in 2006 for her volunteerism.

Did she think that collecting socks at her party in 2002 would lead to a non-profit organization? "Honestly, I had no idea," she says. "I decided to collect a few pairs of socks and give them away at a local shelter." The outpouring of socks was so enormous that Shannon distributes them each Thanksgiving in New York City at the St. Francis of Assisi Church breadline in Manhattan, the church where Mychal served. When a man on the breadline asked Shannon's grandmother if any underwear was available, Shannon began to collect underwear along with the socks.

Shannon remembers: "A homeless man actually asked my mom for underwear. On our trip home from NYC after distributing socks, my mom announced, 'I know what I want for my birthday in March: men's underwear.' Blessed Bloomers was born and we have returned to the streets of NYC every year on the anniversary of 9/11 with underwear packaged discreetly."

"It seems that every time we were there, we said we could do more. When you see the need, it's humbling. That's how Mychal's Message was created."

While Shannon was only 11 on September 11, 2001, she said the event made her who she is today: "I've grown so much since then. At the time, I didn't understand what had happened. It was hard to grasp and deal with it. I was so confused and angry.

"Today, the anger has gone away, and while I still miss Father Mychal, I'm more mature and have come to know a better way to live my everyday life."

The organization that Shannon started when she was just a child has shaped who she is today. She notes: "Mychal's Message is so important to me. There's so much need in the world, especially with homelessness growing. When you're on the New York City breadline at 7 a.m. and you see 300 men standing in line for a sandwich and coffee, and it's a freezing-cold morning and you're wearing three layers of clothes and you see a man in a short-sleeve T-shirt, you can't walk away."

How has September 11 impacted Shannon's young life? "If I can help the life of one person, that's all that matters to me. Through Mychal's Message, I have helped those who need help."

Peter Gudaitis

74

# CHAPTER 11

## A Change of Vocation: Peter Gudaitis

*President, Board of Directors, National Disaster Interfaiths Network*

If Peter Gudaitis, M.Div., has his way, all places of worship in every faith community will be fully prepared to help their members when a disaster — natural or manmade — occurs.

The president of the board of the National Disaster Interfaiths Network (NDIN) has learned that church agencies were the ones that people turned to the most after September 11 and Hurricane Katrina. They were also the agencies that remained open the longest, far after help from the government organizations ended. Peter was executive director of one of those agencies, the New York Disaster Interfaith Services, and saw firsthand how people could get help when no other assistance was offered.

Now, through NDIN, Peter is committed to helping interfaith communities not be taken by surprise as they were after September 11, and preparing members to be resilient and strong in the face of disaster. That was a hard lesson to learn, Peter says, since the New York City interfaith community wasn't organized to respond on September 11.

"In New York City," he says, "we had no disaster response program because we don't get hurricanes, tornadoes, and huge floods like they do in the Midwest.

September 11 was completely unique in terms of trauma and disaster ministry, something we hadn't seen before."

Peter was one of the early organizers of the faith communities in New York City, learning the ropes of disaster recovery in a sort of baptism-by-fire, he says. Having witnessed first-hand how unprepared the Church was, today he is firmly committed to his philosophy that interfaith communities need to be prepared for disasters.

"Disasters cause the most harm to the vulnerable," he says. "Those are our people in the Church. The time to teach them how to be prepared is not after they've lost their home, but before."

While he's familiar with the saying, "life is too short," Peter says he definitely doesn't want life to be quick. He has a lot more work to do. "I know this is important work because I know how I was affected by 9/11. I can help communities so that disasters don't have as much of an impact. The time to do this is before the disaster. The way to do this is to look at the hazards facing your community before they happen."

Peter could relate to folks who lost their homes after September 11. He was forced to evacuate his apartment only blocks away from Ground Zero, temporarily relocating to New Jersey while the apartment was cleaned of the dust, smoke and debris. "You measured how soon you might be going back to the apartment by how much smoke was pouring out of the Ground Zero hole," he recalls.

At the time, Peter was associate director of Episcopal Charities in New York City, a job that positioned him for a leadership role in interfaith disaster recovery after September 11.

With a seminary degree and several years under his belt as a college chaplain at Sewanee, The University of the South in Sewanee, Tennessee, the Connecticut native had returned to the New York area before September 11.

With a heart for service since he was a teenager, Peter's background working with young people, congregations, and social ministry landed him the job at Episcopal Charities in upper Manhattan. At first, he was doing typical church charity work administering a foundation that funded faith-based social service and youth programs. But September 11 changed all that. He was on the job only a month before he was asked to oversee one of the largest relief efforts the Episcopal Church had ever handled.

"Twenty-four hours after 9/11, this type of disaster work was in my portfolio. I found myself managing a $3 million program for disaster recovery. It wasn't planned. It was baptism by fire," he says.

"The New York Diocese and Episcopal Charities decided this wasn't business as usual, and we had to set up structures to deal with a disaster of this magnitude."

The Episcopal Church wasn't the only church body with donations streaming in. The Lutheran Church, Presbyterian Church, and many others found themselves the recipients of millions of dollars very quickly. In addition to funding from the national church offices, people from all over the world were contributing and funds were building. Churches needed a structure and process for distributing money to those in need. "Week Number 1, it was $50,000," says Peter. "Six months later it was $1 million, the next year was $3 million. It continually scaled up."

With help from FEMA, within six months Peter and his colleagues from other denominations started the Unmet Needs Roundtable, a group of organizations with money to give. Each week, the Roundtable would hear the cases of those affected by September 11 for whom there was no other financial help. Episcopal Charities was one of the first agencies to join the Roundtable, along with Lutheran Disaster Response of New York. Peter served on the steering committee. "I knew what it meant for these people. I myself didn't have a home."

The Roundtable members took their roles very seriously. Says Peter, "We were all traumatized by 9/11 and heavily burdened by what happened to all of us. We took very seriously how we were called to help."

The Unmet Needs Roundtable was the longest surviving resource for the 9/11 community, says Peter, only closing its doors in 2009.

With the Roundtable up and running, leaders of the interfaith communities turned their thoughts to organizing an official group that would band them together as a 501(c)(3) non-profit agency. This was the early beginning of New York Disaster Interfaith Services (NYDIS).

"It took a year from the founding of the Roundtable for us to incorporate, but we did it," says Peter. This would be the first time that interfaith agencies in New York City would run a non-profit to aid those affected by September 11.

"When we decided to form NYDIS, I was asked to chair the strategic planning process to set up bylaws and so forth, since I had the background. I was asked to lead the organization. I was trusted with this," he recalls.

Peter saw his role as executive director of NYDIS as being a voice for the lost and forgotten: "A lot of the minority faith community people didn't feel that they had a voice, so we helped give them a voice. This was about equal voice. We all needed one seat at the table."

It was also about playing in the big leagues and holding their own with other larger governmental and social services agencies. "It was hard for the small faith communities to get a seat at the table. It was one more reason to form our own network," he adds.

"All of us perceived ourselves as the underdogs, especially since we were told by many of the big agencies that they would tell us what to do."

Peter, however, had other ideas for NYDIS. "I always thought that I was the little guy," he says. "I grew up as kind of a dorky kid who sometimes fit in and sometimes didn't. I had a passion for service and was involved in my church. I belonged to band and chorus, Boy Scouts. I was the Glee Club generation. I grew up feeling like the little guy and valuing the contribution that I could make to social change. I grew up in a family and a church that valued community service. Helping others was part of my DNA, and it became part of my vocation."

In addition to having a heart for helping others, Peter had what it took to deal with crisis. "I certainly was comfortable in crisis and familiar with best practices for how to fund and run effective programs. No one could have predicted the scale of 9/11. We were flying by the seat of our pants."

While many predicted that the affects of September 11 would be over in a year, Peter and his interfaith colleagues understood that disaster recovery would be long-term.

In addition to being in totally new territory, part of the problem, says Peter, was the fact that the interfaith communities were new to the morass of red tape associated with applying for assistance from governmental agencies. But with NYDIS and the Roundtable, he said, "People came in and said, 'I lost my job; can't pay my mortgage,' and we'd pay it."

A bond was forming among the agencies and NYDIS was quickly becoming the face of the interfaith response to September 11. Peter says, "We used the bond we formed in the crisis as a way to support each other. We gathered around people who were equally as passionate as and even more skilled than we were."

NYDIS was in a position to begin building a long-term strategy for how interfaith communities would respond to disaster, and by September 2003 the agency had grown to 32 employees with a $3.4 million budget.

Peter remembers, "We had Volunteers in Service to America (VISTA), became an AmeriCorps site, and were running the Roundtable. We were the last man standing. Every time a community-based organization closed, we picked up its clients."

NYDIS was also emerging as the go-to disaster preparedness resource for churches. "Fairly early on, we began to recognize that pastors needed to focus on self-care to manage the long-term recovery," he says. "We recognized that part of our mission was about mitigation and healing. We couldn't recover until we had a strategy to deal with potential threats to the community. NYDIS would become a permanent partner for faith communities to develop a more resilient community."

NYDIS's evolution didn't come without growing pains. Says Peter, "The growth of NYDIS was done on a learning curve that we shared together. We built one of the most effective long-term recovery agencies in the country. Ten years later, it was one of the longest surviving long-term agencies and the largest disaster interfaith community."

NYDIS received grants to create mitigation, education, and preparedness training initiatives and developed programs that were used all over the country.

As the agency headed into 2005, NYDIS hit its stride and had many resources and grants, according to Peter. Then Katrina happened and NYDIS quickly became a resource for the disaster in the Gulf region. Peter was asked to speak at conferences to help other interfaith communities organize themselves as NYDIS had.

His message was consistent: "If you focus on skill-building around resilience and develop a skill set for how to take care of yourself and people traumatized in your church community, the affects will be lessened.

"September 11 was a catalyst for changing how faith communities deal with disasters. NYDIS wasn't about giving out money. It was about building resilient communities and about building capacity for resilience and mitigation."

Peter left NYDIS in 2009 and saw that moment, again, as another personal turning point. He considered becoming ordained, but decided he was geared more for social work than being a pastor. "I was drawn more to social services than to a pastoral role for a lot of reasons, and I thought about what would be next for me. September 11 happened and propelled me to my disaster preparedness work. Some would say that the Holy Spirit led me to this, but I don't usually talk like that. I say it was simply an organic process that I was swept up in."

Along with colleagues in interfaith disaster preparedness from around the country, Peter created the idea for National Disaster Interfaiths Network (NDIN), of which he is president of the board. The organization is a national network of disaster interfaith organizations working together to reduce disaster-caused human suffering through the exchange of information and cooperative support. Through consulting, a speakers' bureau, training services, and online resources, NDIN is the continuation of Peter's mission to make sure all faith communities are prepared to build resilient communities before disaster strikes.

"We decided to join together to archive and save the institutional knowledge of 9/11," he says. "We have mentors, tools, database templates, and resources all developed to change the way faith communities interact. We want to stop leaving it to chance."

This is another unmet need that Peter is now fulfilling: "If you're a priest in Gulfport, Mississippi, you should have a good understanding of mitigation for your congregation. I don't think clergy look at their formation for ministry in terms of those opportunities for dealing with trauma. In that sense, they are failing their congregations. Seminaries aren't teaching this."

"We seem to have this bizarre culture in the United States, where when a crisis happens you give big. You send your checks, give out the money, and then move on."

It would be nice if healing worked that way, he says. "In a lot of ways, we have a flawed strategy for responding to crisis. Government entitlements aren't enough and what interfaith agencies provide isn't enough either. We do certain things incredibly well, but just not enough sometimes. September 11 and Katrina are the perfect examples.

"Just look at New York City. We still have thousands of people in need of mental health care. Over 40,000 recovery workers are in medical monitoring or getting settlement money for their ill health. We're not over 9/11 — not by a long shot and not by the tens of thousands of people."

It's a sense that people perceive September 11 as being over that worries Peter most. "Early on, and even through 2007, because of the catastrophic scale of 9/11 with Hurricane Katrina right behind it, there was a lot of memory and history about these events. But this has dissipated now and that worries me."

As Peter looks back on his career over the past ten years, he sees it as a total transformation. "If you had told me ten years ago that I would care about this," he says, "I would have never thought it."

He knows that this goal of advocating for disaster preparedness within the Church will take more time and fortunately, because of September 11, he has learned to be patient. At the same time, he says, he has a new sense of urgency.

"My values have also changed," he says. "Some things I thought were important aren't as important anymore. I'm a wounded warrior. The trauma of leading people in a crisis is something that changes your world view. I'm much more vocal about injustice and inequities now. I'm more intentionally inclusive of people. I'm more patient about some things because they're not important."

"We get caught up in pettiness and we don't often look at big picture. This is the big picture — these are our values, our faith, and what is important. We have to let people know what is critical."

"I also find that the liturgy speaks to me differently. I see things differently now, and as a Christian, I understand things in different ways."

In a way, he is a pioneer in U.S. interfaith disaster preparedness efforts. Colleges now offer advanced degrees in disaster management, and the New York Archdiocese of the Catholic Church has employed disaster recovery personnel since September 11, according to Peter. A colleague from his Episcopal church also teaches a course at Lutheran Theological Seminary in Philadelphia.

"A master's degree in emergency management didn't even exist ten years ago," Peter smiles.

"I think I'm the face of this to some extent. Even still, all these years later, it's humbling to know that I was there. It's amazing to look back over a ten-year period and realize that it was amazing how much we accomplished."

"My life was completely transformed by two and a half hours on 9/11."

Valerie Ghent

# CHAPTER 12

## A Change of Tempo: Valerie Ghent

*Musician and Founder of* Feel the Music!

*Show My Love*
There's no more time for hiding
no more time for pain
no more time for lying
no more time for blame
no more time for grudges, no
I'm gonna show my love

. . .

there's no more time for fighting
no more time for war
no more time for battlefields
cause we're closing every door
no more time for dying
I'm gonna show my love

. . . .

show my love - yes I will
and if there's no more time for teaching
no more time to give
and no more time for children
then there's no more time to live
no more time god can find
I'm gonna show my love

. . .

show my love
show it every day
show my love
show it in every way
show my love

*© 2003 Valerie Ghent, Cavos Music/ASCAP*

These original lyrics pretty much sum up the outlook of singer-songwriter Valerie Ghent after September 11.

Longtime keyboardist, vocalist, and recording engineer with renowned musicians Ashford and Simpson, Valerie has toured and performed with Deborah Harry (Blondie), Billy Preston, Maya Angelou, T.M. Stevens, Grayson Hugh and others. Yet, in many ways, none of this work was as transformative as her nine-month volunteer efforts at the World Trade Center site after September 11.

Valerie's experiences working firsthand with first responders, survivors, and families led her to found *Feel the Music!*, a non-profit organization that brings music and inspiration to children and adults impacted by trauma, loss and illness. "I believe music, in and of itself, has transformative powers for people, and especially for those impacted by trauma," she says. "Singing, playing the drums, or writing a song all release something deep inside. Making music brings you to the heart of the moment — and it brings people together."

*Feel the Music!* began offering programs in 2005 and incorporated as a 501(c)(3) two years later. "When people come together and sing, they heal," she says.

Like many musicians, Valerie found music to be a crucial form of support in difficult times. Through a convergence of events — including her volunteer work at Ground Zero and running an ongoing songwriter's night — Valerie came to realize that music could help families impacted by September 11 heal.

Valerie, a native New Yorker, was in her apartment in the West Village when the planes hit. She recalls being home that day because her apartment was being painted. She remembers, "A friend called and told me to look outside.

I rushed to the window and saw the first tower aflame. Initially, like most people, I thought it was a terrible accident."

"My first impulse was to jump on my bike and head downtown. Instead, I went to the roof with my camera. As the second plane hit, the reality of what was happening hit me. I remember thinking this is it. When the first tower fell, I thought there must have been bombs in the building to bring it down so fast, and when I saw the cloud I thought they were nuclear."

"I really believed it was the end, especially for all of us close enough to see it with our own eyes."

Today, *Feel the Music!* works with hundreds of people each year in the greater New York City metropolitan area, offering workshops in percussion, singing, songwriting, guitar, concerts, retreats, and other unique programs. Says Valerie, "The shock of 9/11 was a wake-up call, a brutal reminder that anything can happen at any time, at any moment, regardless of the lives we are creating for ourselves. Life is so short and can be interrupted when we least expect it."

*Feel the Music!* debuted in Europe in 2010 offering a program in Belfast, Northern Ireland, and creating a chorus of teens impacted by terrorism from around the world. The camp was held in partnership with Project Common Bond, which brings together 70 teens from countries such as Spain, Israel, Palestine, Northern Ireland, the Republic of Ireland and the United States each summer.

"I wanted to do something more with my life than just play gigs and make records," says Valerie. "I feel strongly that musicians and artists have a responsibility to society." *Feel the Music!* has provided the opportunity to give back and to use her music for something meaningful. "I think part of me was looking for that for a long time."

The daughter of musicians — her father was a composer and psychiatrist and her mother a professional violist, composer, and teacher — Valerie understood through her growing-up years that music could completely transform difficult emotional situations. "*Feel the Music!* brings together much of what I learned from my parents," she says. "They constantly encouraged creativity in everything they did."

Both of Valerie's parents died early and unexpected deaths in the years after September 11, her dad in 2003 and her mother in 2006. "Losing both my parents was devastating. My father died during the development of what would become *Feel the Music!,* and my mother died in our first year of running the program. The sheer finality of their deaths strengthened my belief in the relevance and importance of music in our lives."

"Music not only helps us 'express the inexpressible,' it also helps us navigate through difficult times and gives us a vehicle to celebrate the miracle of being alive. My experience as a 9/11 volunteer showed me, more than anything, the power of humanity, the power people have to come together and support one another in the face of overwhelming tragedy and loss."

At the time of September 11, 2001, Valerie was working on her records and had several tours planned, but the attacks shut down everything in New York, including the music industry, and many of her projects were canceled. Finding herself with time on her hands and a desire to help, on September 14 she went to Pier 40 on the Hudson River to volunteer with those who were organizing and managing supplies.

At first, she recalls being told repeatedly, "We don't need any help." After a number of visits, someone finally asked, "Hey can you move those boxes?" That was the beginning of her volunteer outreach at Ground Zero.

Because she had an extensive email list for the music industry, Valerie contacted her musician friends and asked them to donate supplies, things like Duct tape, inhalants, respirators, and boots. "Sometimes I'd ride down to the Ground Zero site on my bike with a pair of boots for someone whose boots had worn through," she says. "People weren't aware of how hot the pile was and how quickly it would destroy boots."

When she wasn't delivering supplies, she helped with logistics with WTC Ground Zero Relief. "People were being flown in from all over the country in two- to three-week shifts for FEMA, the Red Cross, the Salvation Army, but no one gave them maps. They had no idea how to get to and from their hotels to the site. So I contacted a map company in Florida that kindly donated hundreds of laminated maps of Manhattan."

She also learned about the power of perseverance. "I learned that we are all capable of far more than we think we are, that with focus, drive and determination, we can accomplish whatever we set our minds to do," she says. "One could say that just witnessing the clearing of the pile, day after day, week after week, month after relentless month, made clear the power of perseverance. It was a task that seemed impossible to complete, yet due to the hard work of so many, eventually it was done."

A musician at heart, Valerie's thoughts always turned to music. She was running a monthly music night called Songwriter's Beat and turned several concerts into fundraisers. "That September, I decided to start concerts to benefit the local firehouses," she recalls. Meanwhile at the site, she met firefighters and police officers who were musicians and poets, many of whom were writing poems and songs to process their grief and loss, as well as the incomprehensible scene they were seeing every day at the WTC site.

Valerie organized a six-month anniversary tribute concert on March 11, 2002, to benefit the relief efforts. "Before I knew it," she smiles, "I had more performers than I could manage, so we held two concerts. I was deeply moved by how fantastic the songs were. Not only were the songs good, they were historically important and written by people who were there."

The 9/11 concerts were so successful that she assembled a book of poems and a CD of songs to raise money for the 9/11 Families' Association, WTC Ground Zero Relief and the Port Authority Police Department Children's Fund. The CD, "We'll Carry On," raised thousands of dollars.

Little did Valerie know that these experiences were the seeds of what would become *Feel the Music!*. "Everything came so naturally," she says. "It was a convergence of being at the site, meeting 9/11 family members, hearing about their kids, and knowing so many musicians who wanted to do something – anything — to help."

One night, riding home on her bike from the site on the West Side Highway, the idea for *Feel the Music!* came to her. She thought, what if we could bring music lessons and instruments to the kids who lost parents? What if we could start classes? After all, she knew firsthand about the power of music to heal and transform. What she had to learn, however, was how to fund the organization, organize the music teachers and write a grant proposal. "I started learning about the non-profit world thanks to my father," she says. "He started several nonprofits and asked me for assistance in the fall of 2002." As music work was slow and it was a delightful way to spend more time with her father, Valerie agreed. Her father died six months later.

She began sharing office space with the September 11 Families' Association and learned about grant opportunities. She wrote a proposal for *Feel the Music!* and landed a major grant from the American Red Cross Recovery Grants Program. "We were the right idea at the right time," she smiles.

With Red Cross funding, Valerie saw her dream materialize. "I didn't know I could write a grant proposal, let alone raise nearly $1 million for a cause. Nor did I know I could found and run a non-profit and manage a six-figure budget with 30 teachers, therapists, and staff on hand. If anyone had ever told me I would be doing such a thing, I would have said, 'You're out of your mind. I don't know how to write a grant.' "

But running a successful non-profit is exactly what she ended up doing. Today *Feel the Music!* offers more programs and outreach than ever, with top musicians such as Bashiri Johnson, a well known New York City percussionist. *Feel the Music!* works with senior centers, schools, and hospitals, and continues to work with the 9/11 community. "My whole goal was bringing people together and inspiring people though music."

"Drumming and songwriting are some of the most popular classes," says Valerie. "Our teachers are engaging, open-hearted, and filled with love." Classes are held at St. Peter's Lutheran Church and at other sites in Manhattan, as well as in locations around Long Island, New Jersey, and the New York City suburbs.

The organization has also branched out to include programs responding to other disasters. For example, 9/11 families and senior citizens hand painted small percussion frogs (wooden musical instruments which sound like a frog) and sent them to victims of the Madrid bombings, Hurricane Katrina, the war in Iraq, and the Haiti earthquake.

Says Valerie, "One of the things 9/11 taught us was that in the back of our minds, we never know what is going to happen. The combination of the 9/11 tragedy and losing both my parents so suddenly showed me how brief our time really is. In the face of that knowledge, I realized all I could do was show my love. And that's how the song was written."

Even though Valerie has had the kinds of success as a musician that most only yearn for, she says that success often felt superficial. "Being on the road touring and playing big stadiums is basically ego-centric, a kind of immediate gratification. Of course it's fun, and I feel fortunate to have had so many wonderful opportunities to perform. But rarely is life on the road intellectually, emotionally, or spiritually satisfying."

Even the exciting release of her first record left her wanting more: "After I released my first CD, I became disillusioned with the music business. It took making a children's CD with my father a few years later to remember that making music is a joy. I started the Songwriter's Beat as a community effort to support performing songwriters. I then started *Feel the Music!* a few years later. There was always a part of me that wanted to help others."

Today, Valerie not only runs *Feel the Music!* and Songwriter's Beat and works as a professional musician and indie artist, she also teaches internal martial arts and Qigong classes. Starting in the 1990s, Valerie began studying Chinese internal martial arts and Qigong, which she calls another important dimension of her life, an additional road to healing. "Martial arts helps me focus my energy," she says. "I have always been interested in the healing aspects of breath, movement, and music."

She adds: "There are many fascinating overlaps. For example, we recently taught a class in the Six Healing Sounds, which I found really helped my singing and breath control. I envision we'll be doing more of this work in the future, both here in New York and overseas."

To satisfy her creative spirit, Valerie has redirected some of her energy from the ongoing day-to-day operations of running *Feel the Music!* to writing, performing, and recording once again, and was planning to release a double CD. And *Feel the Music!* is transforming to a broader scope.

Valerie says, "I love being in the moment with the kids playing drums or writing songs. When a choir learns a new song, when a senior reads a first lyric, when we bring kids to record their own songs — those are moments I live for. Although we've been successful so far, running the back-end of a non-profit is not my forte. So I'm constantly looking for skilled people who have the knowledge and experience to help *Feel the Music!* thrive and grow."

Valerie has also been researching her family genealogy, and recently reconnected with long-lost family on her mother's side in France, Italy, and Russia. "We have a long line of Italian, Russian, and French composers, artists and architects," she says, "many of whom were involved with the arts and encouraging creativity. I guess music and the calling I feel to do this work is in my blood."

"A number of events have happened in my life since September 11 that now feel like I'm touching something larger than myself. Call it universal life force, natural energy, or spirit. So many things have opened my eyes. They can't all be coincidences."

Being involved in September 11 and starting a non-profit to bring music and creativity to people has helped connect her to a larger vision. "I see life as a gift, a tremendous source of joy and inspiration. Beauty lies within everything. We just have to look."

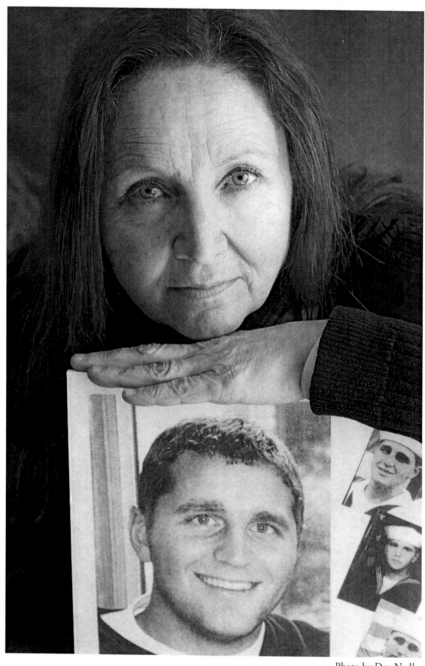

Photo by Dru Nadler

Jean Mariano

# CHAPTER 13

*Remembering: Jean Mariano*

Coordinator, Wreaths Across America

While many of the people in this book were transformed by September 11, 2001, life changed for Jean Mariano on July 6, 2007.

Jean, of New Milford, Connecticut, lost her only son, age 30, in the line of duty in Operation Iraqi Freedom. Not everyone who lost his or her life as a result of September 11 died on that day. Others were killed keeping America safe afterwards.

Chief Petty Officer 1st Class Jason Lewis of Brookfield, Connecticut, shipped out to Iraq in March 2007. He was so proud to represent his country as a Navy Seal in the war on terrorism, says his mom.

"All Jason ever wanted to be, since high school, was a Navy Seal," she says. "I asked him what Plan B was, but there was never a Plan B."

She lost her son, who was handsome, friendly, and a great husband and dad, less than three months after he went overseas. Jason died when a homemade bomb detonated under the Humvee he was riding in.

The only information that the special warfare operator first-class ever told his family was that he was "getting bad guys," says Jean. He wanted to "get the job done," and return home.

Jean, who was very close to her only son, has struggled with her loss, as any mother would, but has found comfort in keeping his memory alive. She has devoted her time to living life to the fullest, just like Jason did, and being a good role model for his three children, Jack, Max and Grace. "I feel that I have to be strong, for his kids, just like Jason would have been."

Although she says she wishes she could just let her guard down and be a grandmother and enjoy the twilight years, she feels that keeping his memory alive is one of her jobs now. "I love to talk about him," she says. "In that special way, I keep his memory alive. I Google his name every day. I have no choice but to."

A quick Google search of his name produces many Web sites memorializing Jason, including Honor the Fallen. Jason is honored for his long-time service in the elite Navy Seals since 1996.

Jean recalls getting the news: "It felt like I was hit by a truck. It takes your breath away."

But life goes on, she says, and now at 58 she finds herself in a new place. She says she tries to be the best she can be for her seven grandchildren, especially teaching Jason's children how to live like their dad lived. "Their father was an incredible guy, and I have to be sure they know that every day. He lived full and hard," says Jean, a trait he inherited from his mom. She honors his memory by doing the same. "I'm not one to say, 'poor me.' I got divorced, we all survived. I've been known to say, 'failure is not a goal.' "

Jason, she says, was never a complainer, so any complaining or feeling sorry for herself is not what Jean does. She works out her grief through a new interest in running, in the spirit of Jason's commitment to fitness. Today, she works out and runs triathlons. "I can't let Jason down."

Jason's memory, she says, reminds her to live life to the fullest. "Life is too short. It's not that I ever thought I needed a bucket list, but in the twinkling of an eye, my priorities are all different now."

Her priorities also call for more travel and taking trips kayaking in Alaska. It's what Jason would want her to do.

Jean has also found comfort in working with the Wreaths Across America project, a non-profit group that raises money to place wreaths on the graves of servicemen. She is the New Milford coordinator for the organization at Center Cemetery in New Milford, where Jason was laid to rest. Working with Remembering Our Veterans, Jean raises money to place holiday wreaths at the cemetery. She usually raises enough to place 300 wreaths. The first one always goes on Jason's grave.

She can often be seen outside stores in town raising money for the cause. "This is something very important to the family and something that I have to do," she says.

She also puts on a Fishing Derby once a year in September at nearby Squantz Pond to keep Jason's memory alive. "I want the children to understand their dad's love of fishing," she says. The Jason D. Lewis Fishing Derby usually raises about $1,000 for charity, mostly through entrance fees and T-shirt sales. Jean plans to continue to expand the derby by selling hot dogs and hamburgers.

"Jason would be so proud of me," she says of her newfound fundraising talents. "If he were here now, he'd look at the Fishing Derby and the Wreaths Across America projects, and say, 'This is so cool.' "

# CHAPTER 14

## Transforming the Future

Almost 3,000 people never got a second chance to make their dreams — however spectacular, however ordinary — happen after 9/11. They were robbed of their lives, and the world was deprived of their gifts.

The reality of so many lives cut short is sad to remember, especially on each anniversary of September 11.

But as much as these stories are heartbreaking, goodness also rose out of September 11. Many New Yorkers stepped back into the light after 9/11 and made the world a better place.

What I've learned from writing about the inspiring people in this book is that we can do anything we set our minds to, at any age. However trite, it's true. We can make a stunning career change like Lisa Orloff, create a fulfilling non-profit organization like KellyAnn Lynch, or become a shamanic healer like Mikki Baloy Davis. The gifts we are given are to be used to make the world a better place. God gives us our gifts to change the future.

I've also come to learn that these gifts don't always have to be used in spectacular ways. I've looked at a framed quote from Mother Theresa on my desk for years, "Do small things with great love." I've seen this quote reflected in the faces of those in these pages. It's OK to make a difference by holding a hometown fishing derby in memory of your son who loved fishing, like Jean Mariano. Or by laying wreaths on soldiers' graves at Christmas. Or by moving your family to a place with a better quality of life, like Jeremy Bouman. Not every action has to save the planet, but every effort will leave a mark on the world. Every positive step, however small, is lasting.

I've also learned that when you take care of yourself, like Chris Conefry did in leaving the rat race of New York for a more laid-back lifestyle, you care for others, too. Putting others first, like Jennifer Adams of the September 11 Families' Association did, returned goodness to her.

What I've also learned from the people in this book is that, for the most part, we're resilient. No matter where each of us was on 9/11, we suffered trauma, too. That day will always be a part of who we are.

Another meaningful lesson is that not everyone is out to make a buck all the time. The 9/11 volunteers looked for nothing in return. New York trauma therapist Dr. David Grand, Ph.D., generously donated his time and expertise to counsel first-responders and relief workers after 9/11 as a way to give back.

The powerful people presented in these pages have given of themselves to make the world a kinder, gentler place. They didn't set out to do this but responded out of their own trauma. Lee Ielpi, president of the September 11 Families' Association, wrote in the foreword to this book how wrong it would be if future generations only had the evil images of towers collapsing and death reports at Ground Zero to define September 11. If they never knew the good that transpired through faith and renewal in the years after, they wouldn't know the whole story.

I hope that in some small way this book has inspired you to "be the change that you want to see in the world," as Mahatma Ghandi advised us. It's our job to affect the future. We always have hope.